HEALTHY MEDITERRANEAN COOKERY

LORRAINE WHITESIDE

Photographs by Amanda Heywood

LITTLE, BROWN AND COMPANY

BOSTON NEW YORK TORONTO LONDON

A LITTLE, BROWN BOOK

First published in the United Kingdom
by Little, Brown and Company (UK) in 1997

Text copyright © 1997 Lorraine Whiteside
The moral right of the author has been asserted

A CIP catalogue for this book is available
from the British Library

ISBN 0 316 88182 1

Typeset by Solidus (Bristol) Limited
Printed and bound in Great Britain by
Clays Ltd, St Ives plc

Little, Brown and Company (UK)
Brettenham House
Lancaster Place
London WC2E 7EN

Lorraine Whiteside is a professional translator and interpreter who has worked and travelled extensively in the various Mediterranean countries. It was while living abroad that she first became interested in food and in the healthy lifestyle enjoyed by the Mediterranean peoples. Her research into the protective nutrients that form the basis of the Mediterranean diet led to this collection of healthy and delicious recipes.

Contents

For my beloved father Eric Whiteside:
treasured memories of you live on in my heart for ever.
Special love to Mum, Daniel, Brian and all my family.

Introduction

Few visitors to the Mediterranean realize that the food they enjoy so much constitutes one of the healthiest diets in the world.

Death rates from coronary heart disease in the UK, USA and Northern Europe are amongst the worst in the world. In the UK, around 330,000 people die from cardiovascular disease each year, accounting for 44 per cent of all deaths.

Mediterranean communities, by comparison, suffer from remarkably low levels of coronary heart disease. France, Spain, Portugal, Greece and Italy have the lowest rates of heart disease of any industrialized nations in the world, beaten only by Japan. They also have a substantially lower risk of developing cancer – the UK's second largest killer disease. Statistics drawn up by the Cancer Research Campaign show that in 1988 cancer accounted for the death of 160,589 people in the UK. In Spain, death rates from cancer during the same period were only 68,069; in Portugal this figure dropped to only 17,196 and in Greece to 18,961. Death rates from cancer in France and Italy were also lower than in the UK.

The Mediterranean people's remarkable immunity to the world's two major health threats is almost certainly linked to their diet. A low intake of harmful saturated fat is in particular credited with the low risk of heart disease and long life-expectancy. Dairy products and red meat, both of which contain high levels of saturated fat, make up only a very small percentage of the Mediterranean diet; they prefer instead to eat pasta, rice, pulses and wholegrain bread, together with fresh vegetables and fruits. Double cream and butter in particular, both laden with saturated fat, are virtually unheard of in the Mediterranean diet. Instead, they prefer olive oil, high in beneficial monounsaturated fat and a recognized blood cholesterol neutralizer.

Saturated fat, extremely low levels of which are consumed in the Mediterranean diet, is now believed to be the major dietary cause of high cholesterol levels, one of the most serious risk factors in the development of coronary heart disease. Most of the cholesterol in the bloodstream is produced by the liver and a diet rich in saturated fat stimulates the liver to increase its production of cholesterol, which is then carried away and deposited on the linings of the arteries, a pattern inevitably leading to atherosclerosis (furring of the arterial walls).

Research has in effect shown that communities with high dietary levels of saturated fat and low dietary levels of fibre are most at risk from developing coronary heart disease, and show an increased incidence of certain types of cancer too.

In addition to the fat factor, the Mediterranean diet is rich in a range of protective nutrients provided by vitamins C, E and beta-carotene, nutrients causing powerful antioxidant activity, a biochemical reaction closely associated with the prevention of cancer.

Medical evidence now shows that the single most important factor in the prevention of serious disease is our diet. In the UK, 70 per cent of deaths are caused by heart disease and cancer, diseases that Mediterranean people have a substantially lower risk of developing.

With its emphasis on high levels of monounsaturated and omega-3 fatty acids, low levels of saturated fat, high levels of complex carbohydrates and antioxidant-rich fresh vegetables and fruits, the Mediterranean diet is now widely recognized as a strong foundation for good health and longevity, and is regarded by many as possibly the healthiest diet in the world.

ANTIOXIDANTS, A KEY PROTECTIVE FORCE

The Mediterranean diet is rich in a range of antioxidant nutrients, derived principally from food sources containing vitamins C, E and beta-carotene (the vegetable form of vitamin A), as well as the trace mineral selenium. Antioxidant nutrients are recognized for their ability to protect the body against the harmful effects of substances known as 'free radicals': destructive, oxygen-free molecules that can cause extensive damage to body cells and tissues.

Free radicals are oxidizing agents formed as a by-product of the body's conversion of food into energy, and also by a number of external factors, including exposure to all kinds of environmental pollutants, inhalation of tobacco smoke and vehicle exhaust fumes and ultra-violet radiation through a damaged ozone layer. Free radicals are highly reactive, unstable molecules. Chemically, they are unpaired electrons which, while searching for an electron to 'mate' with and achieve stability, can ravage body cells and tissues, breaking down the body's auto-immune system and leaving the path wide open to heart disease, cancer and other degenerative diseases. Free radical attack is also believed to be a contributory factor in premature ageing.

Food sources that are rich in antioxidant nutrients, however, play a key role in protecting the body cells against the destructive effects of free radicals. The Mediterranean diet provides high levels of these important antioxidant nutrients, derived in particular from a high intake of fresh fruit, vegetables and whole grains, contributing to a large extent to the low rates of cancer and heart disease.

FOODS WITH A HIGH CONCENTRATION OF ANTIOXIDANT NUTRIENTS

Antioxidant Carotenoids [notably Beta-Carotene]:	Antioxidant Vitamin C:	Antioxidant Vitamin E:
Carrots	Red peppers	Wholegrain breads
Spinach	Green peppers	and cereals
Broccoli	Yellow peppers	Nuts such as pine
Tomatoes	Citrus fruit	nuts and almonds
Watercress	Strawberries	Green leafy vegetables
Peppers	Tomatoes	Olives and extra
Peaches	Potatoes	virgin olive oil
Mangoes		Oily fish
		Asparagus

LIVE-LONGER GOALS OF THE MEDITERRANEAN DIET

The aim of *Healthy Mediterranean Cookery* is to help you to live a longer and more healthy life by adopting a pattern of simple dietary measures that will:

Reduce your risk of contracting the world's two biggest health threats, heart disease and cancer.

Lower your blood cholesterol and blood pressure levels naturally by substantially reducing your intake of unhealthy saturated fats and increasing your intake of healthy mono-unsaturated and omega-3 fatty acids.

Reduce the damage caused to body cells and tissues by free radicals, by increasing your intake of the antioxidant vitamins C, E and beta-carotene through making fresh fruit and vegetables and whole grains a major part of your diet.

Protect your health by eating more oily fish, more complex carbohydrates in the form of wholegrain breads, pulses, pasta and rice, more deeply pigmented vegetables and fruits such as red peppers, spinach, broccoli, carrots, tomatoes, oranges, strawberries and mangoes, and by increasing your intake of all the Mediterranean 'superfoods'.

MEDITERRANEAN SUPERFOODS

OLIVE OIL

In the Mediterranean, olive oil flows like wine, and it is hardly surprising to find that 70 per cent of the total dietary fat consumed in those regions is derived from this healthy oil. With its wonderful, aromatic flavour and great culinary versatility, it is hard to believe that a simple oil could have such amazing health-giving properties. But it does. Olive oil is in fact a rich source of monounsaturated fat which, unlike the saturated fat contained in butter and lard, is actually good for the health of the heart and circulation.

In cholesterol terms, there are both destructive and protective factors: low-density lipoproteins (LDLs) are a destructive type of blood cholesterol, high levels of which can clog the arteries, leading to unhealthy build-ups of arterial plaque; high-density lipoproteins (HDLs), are a protective type of blood cholesterol which can actively assist in breaking up these dangerous deposits in the blood-stream, transporting unwanted cholesterol away from the coronary arteries, to be disposed of by the liver.

The high concentration of monounsaturated fatty acids present in olive oil offers powerful protection for the cardio-vascular system by bringing down raised levels of harmful LDL blood cholesterol and increasing the level of beneficial HDL cholesterol in the bloodstream, thereby establishing a healthy LDL/HDL ratio, a factor that is known to play a key role in the prevention of coronary heart disease.

Olive oil also provides valuable amounts of vitamin E, one of the most effective antioxidant nutrients, widely recognized as an important blood-thinning agent that can help to reduce the risk of thrombosis and protect the heart against the onset of disease.

To obtain maximum health benefits from the oil, always choose extra virgin olive oil, extracted from the first cold-pressing of the finest quality olives and containing the largest proportion of unrefined nutrients.

GARLIC

The Mediterranean people's love affair with garlic is well known - its unique flavour has made it an essential part of Mediterranean cuisine. But garlic also protects the Mediterranean people against the high risk of heart disease and cancer.

1. As an anticoagulant and antithrombotic agent, garlic can thin the blood and discourage the formation of blood clots leading to coronary thrombosis and strokes.
2. One of the active compounds present in garlic, known as allyl disulphide, is believed to have a beneficial effect on blood cholesterol levels, reducing raised levels of the harmful type of LDL blood cholesterol, which carries the most risk of disease, while increasing the level of protective HDL cholesterol in the bloodstream.
3. With antihypertensive properties, garlic can play an important part in reducing raised blood pressure levels. As a vasodilator, garlic may have a dilatory effect on blood vessels, widening the channels and enabling the blood to flow more freely.
4. Research has also shown that garlic has strong antioxidant powers, making it not just a heart food, but a nutrient with anti-carcinogen potential as well. In the USA, the National Cancer Institute places garlic high on the list of 'foods that prevent cancer', and there is increasing evidence that people with a passion for garlic have a significantly lower risk of developing cancer.

OILY FISH

The Mediterranean diet is characterized by an extremely high intake of oily fish such as sardines, mackerel, herrings, salmon and tuna. Oils derived from this type of fish have a substantial concentration of omega-3 fatty acids, a group of essential long-chain polyunsaturates that are highly beneficial to the health of the cardiovascular system.

Protective omega-3 fatty acids are not produced by the fish themselves, but are actually drawn from the plankton on which the fish feed, and stored as polyunsaturated fatty acids in their oily flesh.

A 100 g/3½ oz portion of oily fish such as that consumed in the Mediterranean diet provides around 2-3g/⅛oz of heart-protecting omega-3 fatty acids. By contrast, white fish such as plaice, haddock and cod provide poor levels of omega-3. Generally speaking, the darker the colour of the flesh, the higher its concentration of omega-3 fatty acids.

The Mediterranean's rate of heart disease is about half that of the UK and the USA, and, statistically, communities that include substantial amounts of fish in their diet have much lower rates of coronary heart disease. The Eskimos, for example, huge fish consumers, have virtually no heart disease. The Japanese people's largely fish-based diet leads them to have the lowest rate of heart disease of any industrialized nation in the world.

A diet rich in omega-3 essential fatty acids is believed to substantially reduce the risk of a heart attack or stroke:

1. They reduce the stickiness of blood platelets, thereby lessening the likelihood of blood clot formation.
2. They can lead to a dramatic fall in the level of tryglycerides in the bloodstream (blood fats), raised levels of which are a high risk factor in heart disease.
3. There is a reduction in blood viscosity, enabling the blood to flow more freely through the arteries.

4. Fish oils can reduce the level of clotting protein in the bloodstream, making the blood less likely to form dangerous clots, while at the same time maintaining normal protection against bleeding when cut.
5. They can improve the stability of the heart-beat, reducing its susceptibility to irregular rhythms, a condition known as arrhythmia, development of which can precipitate a heart attack.

TOMATOES

Only recently has the humble red tomato emerged as a star defender in the anti-cancer war. The tomato features extensively in the Mediterranean kitchen, used both as a colourful raw ingredient in salads, and as a delicious cooked ingredient in pasta and rice dishes.

The tomato's key protective force is derived from its high concentration of carotenoids. These carotenoids are the real arch-enemies of the destructive excess free radicals, neutralizing the potentially harmful oxidizing effects, and assisting in preventing cell mutations that can lead to cancer.

Extensive research has revealed that there is a close link between a high consumption of tomatoes and a low occurrence of certain types of cancer. American studies suggest that eating tomatoes at least 10 times a week may reduce the risk of development of some forms of cancer by as much as 50 per cent.

RED PEPPERS

In the cuisine of Southern Italy, France and Spain, the sweet red pepper is used in many ways, appearing extensively in both salads and hot dishes.

A lesser known fact is that the red pepper is one of the richest vegetable sources of antioxidant vitamin C. Weight for weight, red peppers contain over three times as much vitamin C as oranges. Red peppers are also an extremely rich source of beta-carotene, responsible for giving the red pepper its deep red pigment.

The healthy antioxidant partnership of vitamin C and beta-carotene, found to an extremely high degree in red peppers, provides the body cells and tissues with powerful protection against the destructive effects of free radicals.

WHOLEGRAIN BREAD

The coarse-textured, wholegrain, country-style bread eaten with almost every meal in the Mediterranean (with not a pat of butter in sight), is an extremely rich source of antioxidant vitamin E, the B complex group of vitamins, fibre and complex carbohydrates.

The benefits of a high-fibre diet are well known, and whole grains are one of the principal dietary sources that supplies a healthy combination of soluble and insoluble fibre. The insoluble fibre in wheat bran works as a bulking agent in the gut, preventing constipation and reducing the risk of serious bowel disorders. Insoluble fibre may also be an important factor in the prevention of cancer of the large intestine. The soluble-type fibre found in whole grains is believed to assist in reducing harmful LDL blood cholesterol levels and may have a regulatory effect on blood glucose levels.

The germ of wholewheat grains contains high levels of vitamin E, considered by many to be the most effective antioxidant vitamin, playing a key role in protecting all the body cells from the damaging effects of oxidation, providing a powerful protective force against heart disease, cancer and premature ageing.

The World Health Organisation has identified a low dietary intake of vitamin E as being a principal risk factor in the development of coronary heart disease. Research undertaken by a team of medical scientists at Cambridge University has revealed that a high intake of vitamin E can actually be more effective than aspirin or cholesterol-lowering drugs, reducing the risk of heart disease by up to 75%.

PASTA, RICE AND PULSES

The Mediterranean diet has a high proportion of complex carbohydrates, starchy nutrients derived from sources such as pasta, rice, pulses, potatoes and wholegrain breads. As much as 70 per cent of the Mediterranean diet is made up of these vital protective nutrients, a high intake of which is combined with a low saturated fat intake.

Complex carbohydrates are energy-fuelling agents, slowly absorbed and digested by the body, inducing a steady, gradual increase in blood glucose levels, an important factor in healthy cell metabolism and blood sugar regulation. They are believed to have a beneficial effect on cholesterol in the bloodstream, reducing the level of destructive LDL cholesterol and increasing the level of protective HDL blood cholesterol, essential to the maintenance of a healthy cardio-vascular system. High levels of complex carbohydrates in the diet are also believed to be associated with a low occurrence of certain types of cancer.

Highly prized in the Mediterranean, pasta, pulses and rice are much undervalued elsewhere and deserve to be given far greater prominence. Following the advice of the World Health Organization, at least half our daily calorie intake should be made up of these complex carbohydrates.

RED WINE

The suggestion that 'wine is the best medicine' continues to attract a great deal of controversy, but controversial or not, abstinence may not after all be good for us, for research has shown that moderate amounts of red wine can actually be beneficial to the health of the heart and immune system. The health-protecting power of red wine is believed to be derived not from its alcohol content, but from its high levels of polyphenols, biologically active antioxidant compounds found in the deeply-pigmented skin of red grapes and passed on to the wine through fermentation.

Statistically, people such as the Mediterraneans who enjoy a tipple or two a day live longer than those who don't. Supported by the British Heart Foundation, increasing evidence now suggests that two or three glasses of red wine a day may help to prevent the onset of coronary heart disease in later life, by assisting in reducing the level of harmful low-density lipoproteins in the bloodstream, raised levels of which are a causative factor in the development of arteriosclerosis (hardening of the arteries) later in life. Red wine may also work as an anticoagulant, thinning the blood and inhibiting the formation of blood clots, substantially reducing the risk of a heart attack or stroke.

Moreover, with its high concentration of antioxidant phenols, moderate amounts of red wine may also offer some protection against cancer. One of the key antioxidants in red wine is gallic acid, a phenolic compound that may help to suppress the formation of nitrosamines, cancer-causing substances formed through a reaction of nitrates with amines, nitrogen compounds found in certain types of preserved and processed foods.

KEEPING YOUNG

Excessive amounts of oxidizing free radicals are believed to be a major factor in cellular ageing, and there is growing evidence to suggest that high levels of antioxidant nutrients, such as those present in the Mediterranean diet, may be able to contribute to a slowing down of the ageing process, by counteracting unwanted oxidation of body cells, resulting from complex free radical activity.

The antioxidant nutrient most closely associated with anti-ageing is vitamin E, a fat-soluble vitamin stored in fatty tissues and in the protective membrane of body cells. Vitamin E suppresses the oxidation of lipids (fatty acids) present in cell membranes, a deteriorative reaction closely linked to ageing.

Another powerful antioxidant nutrient, vitamin C, is essential for the formation of collagen, which assists in binding cells together, keeping the skin firm and supple. Low levels of collagen resulting from a vitamin C deficiency may be implicated in undue wrinkling and sagging of skin tissue.

Millions of pounds are spent each year on the quest for eternal youth, with collagen implants and expensive vitamin E-based skincare products constituting a large part of that multi-million pound industry. A high dietary concentration of antioxidant nutrients as consumed in the Mediterranean regions may however be a more natural and less expensive way of pursuing this quest. And while we recognize that the fountain of eternal youth is biologically unattainable, it is apparent that the Mediterranean diet may be able to make a major contribution to delaying the onset of cellular ageing, helping to keep our body cells young and healthy for as long as is biologically possible.

NOTES ON FISH PREPARATION

Sardines and Mullet

To bone a sardine, first scrape off the scales with a small sharp knife, holding the fish under cold running water. Cut off the head and tail (some recipes leave the heads on). Cut the sardine along the belly and remove the innards. Lay the sardine down flat, skin side up, and press firmly along the backbone with your thumb, to loosen it. Turn the fish over and use a sharp knife to prise out the backbone from head to tail in one piece. Remove any stray bones with tweezers.

Squid

The edible parts of a squid are the body and tentacles. To clean squid, first pull off the head and tentacles, holding the body firmly with one hand. Most of the innards will come away with the head. Cut off the tentacles and discard the head. Remove the ink sacs, transparent quill and any remaining innards and rinse the body cavity under cold running water. With a knife, scrape off the thin skin on the body and rinse again.

Mussels

Wash well under cold running water and scrub the shells, scraping offf any encrustations. Pull off the 'beards' and rinse again. Discard any shells that are broken, or that do not close swiftly when tapped.

Scallops

Choose large firm shells. To open, insert a short, sharp knife between the shells at the rounded part and twist hard. Remove the greyish fringe around the scallop.

NOTES ON MEASUREMENTS

Recipes give measurements in both metric and imperial units. For greatest accuracy, follow one system or the other, rather than alternating between both, for each recipe you use.

Tablespoons

The recipes use a 15 ml tablespoon. All dry ingredients are measured in rounded tablespoons unless 'level' is stated. Two tablespoons of liquid ingredients correspond to 30 ml/1 fl oz.

Teaspoons

Teaspoons hold 5 ml and are always level.

Cup Measures

Some cooks, especially in the US, use volume (cup) rather than weight measures. The following weight-to-cup equi-valents are designed to help these cooks. The cup used is an

American one, which holds 8 fl oz (16 × 15 ml tablespoons/ approximately 250 ml).

CONVERSION TABLES

Liquid Measurements

50 ml	2 fl oz	¼ cup
90 ml	3 fl oz	⅓ cup
125 ml	4 fl oz	½ cup
150 ml	¼ pint	⅔ cup
175 ml	6 fl oz	¾ cup
250 ml	8 fl oz	1 cup
350 ml	12 fl oz	1½ cups
500 ml	16 fl oz	2 cups
600 ml	1 pint	2½ cups
750 ml	1¼ pints	3 cups
900 ml	1½ pints	3½ cups

Flour

60 g	2 oz	½ cup
125 g	4 oz	1 cup
175 g	6 oz	1½ cups
500 g	1 lb	4 cups

Sugar

30 g	1 oz	2 tbsp
125 g	4 oz	½ cup
250 g	8 oz	1 cup

Grated cheese

30 g	1 oz	¼ cup

Rice

125 g	4 oz	½ cup

Soft fruit (raspberries, strawberries)

125 g	4 oz	1 cup

Nuts (pine nuts, chopped walnuts, slivered almonds)

125 g	4 oz	1 cup

1
Soups

ZUPPA DI POMODORO ALLA FIORENTINA

TOMATO AND BASIL SOUP WITH BLACK OLIVE CROSTINI

The perfect partnership of tomatoes and basil reaches sublime heights in this luscious soup, with the added flavours of fennel, garlic and olive oil making it altogether a very healthy combination. Tomatoes are an excellent source of antioxidant vitamins beta-carotene and vitamin C.

SERVES 4–6

100 ml / 3 1/2 fl oz extra virgin olive oil
2 large onions, finely chopped
1 fennel bulb, finely chopped
4 cloves garlic, finely chopped
150 ml / 1/4 pint dry white wine
2 large bunches of basil, leaves picked and stems reserved
2 kg / 4lb ripe plum tomatoes, skinned, seeded and coarsely chopped
1 sprig of fresh thyme
1 bay leaf
600 ml / 1 pint vegetable stock
1 tablespoon caster sugar
freshly ground sea salt and black pepper
Black Olive and Garlic Crostini (see page 30), to serve

Warm 4 tablespoons of olive oil in a large saucepan. Add the onions, fennel and garlic and sweat over a low heat for about 6 minutes, until soft and translucent, but not coloured. Pour in the white wine and simmer over a moderate heat until reduced by half.

Add the tomatoes to the pan together with the basil stems, thyme and bay leaf. Pour in the vegetable stock, add the sugar, then season with salt and pepper. Simmer over a moderate heat for about 12 minutes.

Remove the basil stems, thyme and bay leaf, then pour the soup into a food processor or blender and process until smooth. Strain through a nylon sieve into a clean saucepan.

Just before serving, coarsely tear the basil leaves and stir into the soup with the remaining olive oil. Serve with crostini.

SOUPE DE COQUILLES SAINT JACQUES A LA PROVENCALE

PROVENÇAL SOUP OF SCALLOPS WITH JULIENNE OF VEGETABLES

Memories of the warm, scented Provençal air come back to me when I taste this exquisite soup. The soup is light, almost like a shellfish jus, and the scallops are just gently poached, so that they retain the wonderful flavour of the sea. Scallops are rich in protein, and very low in fat.

SERVES 4

2 tablespoons extra virgin olive oil
2 large carrots, cut into julienne strips
1 fennel bulb, cut into julienne strips
1 large leek, cut into julienne strips
90 ml / 3 fl oz dry white vermouth
2 teaspoons freshly squeezed lemon juice
600 ml / 1 pint fish stock, reduced over a moderate heat to
450 ml / 3/4 pint
8 scallops with corals
freshly ground sea salt and black pepper
1 tablespoon chopped chives

Warm the oil in a large saucepan, then add the vegetables. Cover and sweat over a low heat for about 3 minutes, until soft, but not coloured. Pour in the vermouth, lemon juice and stock, and simmer for 5 minutes.

Slice the white part of each scallop in half, then season the scallops and corals with salt and pepper. Add to the vegetables and simmer over a moderate heat for 1 minute only – it is essential that the scallops are only briefly poached as over-cooking will make them tough. Remove from the heat and serve the soup at once, sprinkled with chopped chives.

CREME DE CAROTTES A LA CORIANDRE

CARROT AND CORIANDER SOUP

A hint of coriander and orange enhances the sweet flavour of carrots in this tasty soup. Unlike most vegetables, carrots provide more nutrients when cooked, as cooking actually releases the carotene in a form that is more readily absorbed by the body. Try to obtain organically grown carrots to eliminate the problem of possible pesticide residues.

SERVES 6

4 tablespoons extra virgin olive oil
1 kg/2 lb carrots, finely chopped
125 g/4 oz shallots, finely chopped
125 g/4 oz leeks, finely chopped
125 g/4 oz potatoes, peeled and finely sliced
2 cloves garlic, finely chopped
1 litre/1¾ pints chicken stock
finely grated zest of ½ orange
freshly ground sea salt and black pepper
2 tablespoons chopped coriander leaves

Warm the oil in a saucepan and add the carrots, shallots, leeks, potatoes and garlic. Cover, then sweat the vegetables over a low heat for 6–8 minutes, until soft and translucent, but not coloured. Pour in the chicken stock, then bring slowly to the boil and simmer for about 15 minutes. Remove from the heat and add the orange zest.

Pour the soup into a food processor or blender and process until smooth. Return to the saucepan, season to taste with salt and pepper, then stir in the chopped coriander. Ladle into warm soup bowls and serve at once.

SOPA DE LENTEJAS

LENTIL SOUP

Lentil soup is popular throughout the Mediterranean, with many regional variations. My own favourite is this Andalusian recipe, a hearty and warming dish that needs nothing more than a chunk of country bread to accompany it.

SERVES 6

2 tablespoons extra virgin olive oil
1 large onion, finely chopped
1 small leek, finely chopped
1 celery stalk, finely chopped
500 g / 1 lb brown lentils
2 cloves garlic, finely chopped
2 teaspoons paprika
1.5 litres / 2$\frac{1}{2}$ pints chicken stock
1 bay leaf
freshly ground sea salt and black pepper
2 tablespoons finely chopped coriander leaves

Warm the oil in a large saucepan, then add the onion, leek and celery. Sweat over a moderate heat until soft and translucent, but not coloured. Stir in the lentils, garlic and paprika. Add the chicken stock and bay leaf, then season. Simmer for about 1 hour, until the lentils are soft.

Remove about one-third of the lentils from the saucepan with a slotted spoon, then pour the soup into a food processor or blender and process until smooth. Return to the saucepan and add the reserved whole lentils to the soup. This combination of puréed and whole lentils gives a nice texture to the soup. Check the seasoning.

Serve piping hot, sprinkled with chopped coriander and accompanied by wholemeal country bread.

GAZPACHO

A taste of Andalusian sun is contained in this wonderful chilled soup, rich in the vibrant Mediterranean flavours of tomatoes, peppers, garlic and olive oil.

SERVES 4-6

1.25 kg/2½ lb tomatoes, skinned, seeded and coarsely chopped
½ cucumber, peeled, seeded and chopped
2 onions, chopped
3 red peppers, cored, seeded and coarsely chopped
3 cloves garlic, chopped
90 g/3 oz Olive Oil Bread (see page 244), crusts removed and cut into small chunks
200 ml/7 fl oz extra virgin olive oil
2 tablespoons sherry vinegar
iced water
freshly ground sea salt and black pepper

GARNISHES
2 tomatoes, skinned, seeded and finely chopped
¼ cucumber, peeled, seeded and finely chopped
1 onion, finely chopped
½ red pepper and ½ green pepper, cored, seeded and finely chopped
60 g/2 oz Garlic Croûtons (see page 35)

Place the tomatoes, cucumber, onions, red peppers, garlic, bread, olive oil and vinegar in a food processor or blender and process until thoroughly amalgamated but not completely smooth. Pour into a large soup tureen and add sufficient iced water to give a thick pouring consistency. Season to taste. Cover and chill for about 2 hours.

Serve with the garnishes in small separate bowls.

CRÈME DE CRESSON

WATERCRESS SOUP

Although not strictly a typical Mediterranean dish, this soup is very popular, and its wonderful peppery flavour certainly does deserve recognition. Watercress is highly nutritious, containing substantial amounts of beta-carotene, vitamin C and the minerals iron and calcium.

SERVES 4

2 tablespoons extra virgin olive oil
3 shallots, finely chopped
250 g / 8 oz potatoes, peeled and thinly sliced
2 cloves garlic, finely chopped
350 g / 12 oz watercress, stalks removed
1 litre / 1³/₄ pints chicken stock
freshly ground sea salt and black pepper
1 tablespoon crème fraîche
blanched watercress leaves, to garnish
Garlic Croûtons (see page 35), to serve

Warm the olive oil in a large saucepan, add the shallots and sauté over a moderate heat until soft and translucent but not coloured. Add the potatoes and garlic and cook over a low heat for 4–5 minutes, until the potatoes are soft.

Add the watercress and cook for a further minute. Pour in the chicken stock and season with salt and pepper. Bring to the boil, cover, then simmer over a moderate heat for about 15 minutes.

Transfer the mixture to a food processor or blender and process until smooth. Strain the soup back into the saucepan, then add the crème fraîche, stirring well until smooth. Garnish the soup with blanched watercress leaves and serve with a generous spoonful of garlic croûtons.

SOPA DE PEREJIL, CANAPES DE ATUN

PARSLEY SOUP WITH TUNA CANAPES

More than just a versatile garnish, parsley is actually a very nutritious little herb. It is an excellent source of iron and folate, and contains useful amounts of those important antioxidant vitamins C and beta-carotene. Eaten raw, parsley works as a natural diuretic and blood purifier. Tuna canapés are a perfect accompaniment to this lovely soup.

SERVES 4

100 ml/3¹/₂ fl oz extra virgin olive oil
4 shallots, finely chopped
1 celery stalk, finely chopped
4 cloves garlic, finely chopped
500 g/1 lb potatoes, peeled and very thinly sliced
200 g/7 oz chopped parsley
1 litre/1³/₄ pints vegetable stock
freshly ground sea salt and black pepper
4 teaspoons crème fraîche
Tuna Canapés (see page 33), to serve

Warm the olive oil in a large saucepan, then add the shallots, celery, garlic and potatoes. Cover and sweat the vegetables over a low heat for about 5 minutes, until soft but not coloured.

Add half the parsley, then pour on the vegetable stock. Simmer over a moderate heat for about 15 minutes, until the vegetables are soft.

Add the remaining parsley to the soup, then pour into a food processor or blender and process until smooth. Return to the pan and season to taste with salt and pepper. Ladle into warm soup bowls and swirl a teaspoon of crème fraîche into each bowl of soup. Serve with tuna canapés.

ZUPPA DI COZZE ALLA NAPOLETANA

NEAPOLITAN MUSSEL SOUP

This substantial soup is typical of the southern Italian style of cooking, particularly the region surrounding Naples, famous for its lavish use of tomatoes, garlic and olive oil. Here the classic Neapolitan sauce is combined with fresh mussels to make a wonderfully flavoured soup. Mussels are rich in the minerals iron and iodine, and are a low-fat source of protein.

SERVES 4

750 g/1½ lb mussels in their shells, scrubbed and beards removed
200 ml/7 fl oz dry white wine
1 onion, finely chopped
1 bouquet garni
1 clove garlic, finely chopped

NEAPOLITAN SAUCE
100 ml/3½ fl oz extra virgin olive oil
3 cloves garlic, finely chopped
1 small chilli pepper, seeded and finely chopped
1.25 kg/2½ lb plum tomatoes, skinned, seeded and coarsely chopped
freshly ground sea salt and black pepper
2 generous handfuls of basil leaves, coarsely torn

Discard any shells that are not tightly closed. Place the scrubbed mussels in a large saucepan with the white wine, onion, bouquet garni and garlic. Cover and simmer over a moderately high heat for about 5 minutes, until all the mussel shells are open.

Remove the mussels from the saucepan, using a slotted spoon, and reserve. Boil the mussel stock over a moderate heat until reduced by half, then strain.

To make the Neapolitan sauce, warm 4 tablespoons of olive oil in a large saucepan, then add the garlic and chilli pepper. Sauté over a low heat for 2–3 minutes so that the oil is well flavoured. Add the tomatoes and season with salt and pepper. Simmer over a moderate heat for about 15 minutes, until the tomatoes are reduced to a thick pulp.

Add the reduced mussel stock to the sauce, together with the remaining olive oil and half the basil leaves. Remove two-thirds of the mussels from their shells, then add to the sauce, together with the unshelled mussels. Discard any mussels that have failed to open. Warm over a moderate heat for a further 2–3 minutes, to allow the flavours to blend together. Serve the soup in deep bowls, sprinkled with the remaining basil leaves.

ZUPPA DI FAGIOLI NERO

BLACK BEAN SOUP WITH RED PEPPER CROSTINI

Black beans make a wonderfully satisfying soup – earthy and aromatic, tempered with the intense flavours of garlic, chilli pepper, coriander and cumin. Black beans and other pulses are an excellent source of many health-giving nutrients. A low-fat source of protein, they also provide both soluble and insoluble fibre and a good helping of the minerals iron and potassium, as well as the B complex group of vitamins.

SERVES 4–6

250 g/8 oz black beans, soaked overnight
4 tablespoons extra virgin olive oil
2 large onions, finely chopped
4 cloves garlic, crushed
1 celery stalk, finely chopped
1 small chilli pepper, seeded and finely chopped
1 teaspoon ground coriander
1 teaspoon ground cumin
1.5 litres/2½ pints vegetable stock
freshly ground sea salt and black pepper
4 teaspoons sour cream
1 tablespoon chopped coriander leaves, to garnish
Red Pepper Crostini (see page 32), to serve

Drain the beans and rinse under cold running water. Warm the olive oil in a large saucepan, then add the onions, garlic, celery and chilli pepper. Cover and sweat over a low heat for about 5 minutes, until soft and translucent, but not coloured. Stir in the coriander and cumin, then add the black beans. Pour in the vegetable stock and simmer gently for about 3 hours, until the beans are tender.

Remove about a quarter of the beans from the saucepan with a slotted spoon and reserve. Pour the soup into a food processor or blender and process until smooth. Return the soup to the pan, stir in the reserved beans, and season to taste with salt and pepper.

Serve the soup piping hot. Swirl a teaspoon of sour cream on each bowl and sprinkle with coriander leaves. Serve a plate of red pepper crostini to accompany the soup.

SOUPE DE MOULES AU FENOUIL ET AU SAFRAN

SAFFRON-SCENTED MUSSEL AND FENNEL SOUP

The fragrant aroma of fennel, the sweet scent of saffron and the rich flavour of the sea are captured in this wonderful soup. With so many nutritious ingredients, the soup is almost a complete meal. The mussels are a great low-fat source of protein, and are rich in iron, zinc, iodine and selenium; the fennel, celery, shallots and leek are packed with essential vitamins and minerals; while the potatoes are a valuable source of complex carbohydrates, providing the body with energy.

SERVES 6

1 kg/2 lb mussels in their shells, scrubbed and beards removed
200 ml/7 fl oz dry white wine
2 shallots, finely chopped
1 clove garlic, crushed
1 teaspoon fennel seeds, tied up in muslin
1 bay leaf

FENNEL AND SAFFRON CREAM
4 tablespoons extra virgin olive oil
1 large fennel bulb, trimmed and finely chopped
2 celery stalks, finely chopped
2 shallots, finely chopped
1 leek, finely chopped
1 clove garlic, crushed
250 g/8 oz potatoes, peeled and thinly sliced
900 ml/1½ pints fish stock
¼ teaspoon saffron threads
freshly ground sea salt and black pepper
2 tablespoons chopped chives

Discard any mussels that are not tighly closed. Place the mussels in a large saucepan with the white wine, shallots, garlic, fennel seeds and bay leaf. Cover and simmer over a moderately high heat for about 5 minutes, until all the mussel shells are open. Discard any that fail to open.

Remove the mussels from the saucepan with a slotted spoon, and reserve. Boil the mussel stock over a moderately high heat until reduced by half, then strain.

To make the fennel and saffron cream, warm the olive oil in a large saucepan, then add the fennel, celery, shallots, leek, garlic and potatoes. Cover and sweat over a low heat for 5–6 minutes, until soft but not coloured. Pour in the fish stock, reduced mussel stock and saffron. Simmer over a moderate heat for about 20 minutes, until the vegetables are tender.

Pour the soup into a food processor or blender and process until smooth. Strain the soup into a clean saucepan and season with salt and pepper to taste. Take the mussels out of their shells and add to the soup. (If you like, leave just a few of the mussels in their shells, to add a typical Mediterranean character to the soup). Warm through for 1–2 minutes, then ladle into warm soup bowls and sprinkle with chopped chives.

SOPA DE AJO

GARLIC SOUP

The original Moorish version of this soup was made, in truly austere fashion, with only garlic, water, salt and bread. In this more sustaining Andalusian recipe, eggs are poached in a beef stock highly flavoured with garlic.

SERVES 6

1.25 litres/2 pints beef stock
18 cloves garlic, peeled but left whole
2 sprigs of rosemary
2 sprigs of thyme
freshly ground sea salt and black pepper
4 tablespoons extra virgin olive oil
6 slices Wholemeal Country Bread, cut into circles (see page 278)
6 eggs

Preheat the oven to 180°C/350°F/Gas Mark 4.

Bring the beef stock to the boil in a large saucepan, then add the garlic cloves, rosemary and thyme. Season with salt and pepper. Simmer over a moderate heat for about 25 minutes, until the garlic is soft and the stock is infused with the flavour of the garlic and herbs.

Meanwhile, drizzle some olive oil over the circles of wholemeal country bread and toast lightly in the preheated oven for about 10 minutes.

At the end of the cooking time, remove the herbs from the stock. Very carefully crack the eggs into the garlic soup and poach gently for about 2 minutes. Lift out the poached eggs with a slotted spoon and drain on kitchen paper.

To serve, place a circle of toasted bread in the bottom of each soup bowl, then place one of the poached eggs on top. Ladle the soup over the eggs and serve at once.

AVGOLEMONO

GREEK EGG AND LEMON SOUP

This classic blend of eggs and lemons appears in many Greek dishes, and is often served as a sauce to accompany meat or chicken. Here the avgolemono is served as a light and delicate soup, flavoured with a good chicken stock. Eggs, a rich source of protein, also provide valuable amounts of vitamin B12 and choline.

SERVES 4

1.25 litres / 2 pints well-flavoured chicken stock
4 tablespoons long-grain rice, rinsed in cold water
3 cloves garlic, crushed
3 eggs
freshly squeezed juice of 2 large lemons, strained
4 slices of lemon, very finely cut, to garnish
4 tablespoons chopped fresh dill, to garnish

Bring the chicken stock to the boil in a large saucepan, then add the rice and garlic. Simmer over a moderate heat for about 10 minutes, until the rice is tender, then remove from the heat.

Beat the eggs until frothy, then gradually beat in the freshly squeezed lemon juice. Stir 3 tablespoons of the hot stock into the egg and lemon mixture, beating continuously, then return the mixture to the pan. Set the soup over a very low heat and whisk constantly for 2–3 minutes, until a light, creamy consistency is obtained. Do not allow the soup to boil, or the eggs will curdle.

Adjust the seasoning if necessary, then ladle into soup bowls. Garnish with thin slices of lemon and a sprinkling of fresh dill.

CREME D'OSEILLE, CROUSTADES PROVENCALES

SORREL SOUP WITH PROVENÇAL CROUSTADES

Sorrel is an outstanding herb, full of flavour and absolutely superb in this soup. Although you are unlikely to find sorrel in your local supermarket, it is very easy to grow outdoors, and certainly makes a welcome addition to a small herb garden. Both sorrel and lettuce contain valuable vitamins and minerals, notably antioxidant vitamin C, iron and folic acid. Homeopaths believe that sorrel can calm the nerves and aid digestion.

Miniature Provençal croustades topped with a blend of black olives, anchovies, capers and garlic make a lovely accompaniment to the soup.

SERVES 4

2 tablespoons extra virgin olive oil
1 large onion, finely chopped
1 celery stalk, finely chopped
1 large potato, peeled and finely sliced
250 g/8 oz sorrel, stalks removed and leaves coarsely torn
250 g/8 oz flat lettuce leaves, roughly torn
3 tablespoons chopped chervil leaves
2 tablespoons dry white vermouth
900 ml/1½ pints chicken stock
2 tablespoons crème fraîche
freshly ground sea salt and black pepper
Provençal Croustades (see page 34), to serve

Warm the olive oil in a large saucepan, then add the onion, celery and potato. Cover and sweat over a low heat for about 5 minutes, until soft and translucent, but not coloured.

Add the sorrel and lettuce leaves to the saucepan. Sprinkle on 2 tablespoons of the chervil and leave to sweat for 1 minute. Pour in the vermouth and simmer for 1 minute, until the vegetables and herbs are reduced to a soft pulp. Now pour in the chicken stock and season with salt and pepper. Simmer over a moderate heat for about 10 minutes.

Pour the soup into a food processor or blender and process until smooth. Strain through a nylon sieve, then return to a clean saucepan. Lightly beat the crème fraîche, then add to the soup, stirring over a low heat, until the soup thickens to a smooth, creamy consistency. Ladle into warm soup bowls and sprinkle with the remaining chopped chervil. Serve the soup accompanied by a platter of Provençal croustades.

SOUPE AU PISTOU

PROVENÇAL VEGETABLE SOUP WITH PISTOU

Soupe au Pistou is a famous Provençal classic, sumptuously laden with haricot beans, French green beans and other wonderful vegetables, flavoured with a sensational, highly perfumed Niçoise paste made with a blend of garlic, basil, tomato, Parmesan and olive oil.

The soup is also highly nutritious. The vegetables are all rich in vitamins and minerals; the haricot beans are a valuable source of protein, B vitamins and fibre; and with its high garlic and olive oil content the pistou supplies both antioxidants and monounsaturated fatty acids.

SERVES 4

175 g/6 oz dried white haricot beans [cannellini are ideal],
soaked overnight with 2 teaspoons bicarbonate of soda
1.25 litres (2 pints) water
freshly ground sea salt and black pepper
250 g/8 oz French green beans, cut diagonally into 1 cm/¹/₂ inch
pieces
2 large leeks, sliced
2 large carrots, finely sliced
2 large courgettes, thickly sliced
1 large potato, peeled and diced
1 bouquet garni

PISTOU
4 large cloves garlic, peeled
2 generous handfuls of basil leaves
1 large grilled tomato, skinned and seeded
4 tablespoons freshly grated Parmesan
4–6 tablespoons extra virgin olive oil

Drain the beans and rinse under cold running water. Place in a large saucepan and cover with cold water. Bring to the boil and simmer over a moderate heat for about 1 hour, until the beans are almost tender, then drain.

In a separate saucepan, bring the measured water to the boil, seasoning with salt and pepper. Add the green beans, leeks, carrots, courgettes, potato, haricot beans and bouquet garni, and simmer over a moderate heat for about 45 minutes, until all the vegetables are tender. Remove the bouquet garni and discard.

Meanwhile, prepare the pistou. Pound the garlic cloves and basil leaves together, using a pestle and mortar. When reduced to a smooth pulp, add the tomato and pound well. Gradually blend in the grated Parmesan and olive oil, adding a small quantity of each alternately, and pounding well after each addition. Add sufficient olive oil to make the pistou into a fairly fluid paste.

You may add the pistou to the soup before serving, but even better, pass it around the table, allowing each person to stir the pistou into the soup and savour the wonderful aroma.

SOUPE DES MAURES

PUMPKIN SOUP

There are many regional variations on pumpkin soup. Some recipes add vermicelli or rice instead of beans, but this Provençal version with cannellini beans is one of the finest.

SERVES 4–6

*125 g / 4 oz dried cannellini beans, soaked overnight with 2
teaspoons bicarbonate of soda
3 tablespoons extra virgin olive oil
3 shallots, finely chopped
1 celery stalk, finely chopped
500 g / 1 lb pumpkin, peeled, seeded and cut into cubes
1.5 litres / 2½ pints vegetable stock
1 bouquet garni
freshly ground sea salt and black pepper*

Drain the beans and rinse under running water. Place in a large saucepan and cover with cold water. Bring to the boil, then simmer for about 1½ hours, until tender, then drain.

Warm the olive oil in a large saucepan, then add the shallots and celery. Sweat over a low heat for about 4 minutes until soft and translucent but not coloured, then add the pumpkin. Cook gently for a further 2–3 minutes, to soften the pumpkin, then pour in 1.25 litres/2 pints of the stock. Add the cooked beans and the bouquet garni, and season with salt and pepper. Cover and simmer for about 25 minutes, until the pumpkin is tender.

Remove and discard the bouquet garni, pour the soup into a food processor or blender, add the remaining stock and process until smooth. Strain into a clean pan, adjust the seasoning and serve piping hot.

PAPPA AL POMODORO

TOMATO AND BREAD SOUP WITH BASIL AND GARLIC

The Italians manage to make good use of day-old bread in a most imaginative way, simply by incorporating it into a classic health-giving mixture of tomatoes, basil, garlic and olive oil. Although called a soup, this really is quite a substantial dish.

SERVES 6

175 ml/6 fl oz extra virgin olive oil, plus extra to taste
4 large cloves garlic, finely chopped
2 kg/4 lb tomatoes, skinned, seeded and coarsely chopped
2 × 1-day-old loaves of Olive Oil Bread (see page 244), crusts removed and broken into chunks
600 ml/1 pint vegetable stock
2 generous handfuls of basil leaves, coarsely torn, plus extra to taste
freshly ground sea salt and black peppper

Warm half the olive oil in a large saucepan and add the chopped garlic. Sauté very gently for about 5 minutes to soften the garlic and release its flavour, but do not allow it to colour. Add the tomatoes and simmer over a moderate heat for about 15 minutes, until reduced to a thick pulp.

Stir the bread into the tomatoes, then pour on the vegetable stock. Season with salt and pepper, then simmer over a low heat for about 10 minutes.

Remove from the heat, add the basil, and stir in the remaining olive oil. Cover and leave to rest for about 5 minutes before serving to enable the flavours to be absorbed by the bread and tomatoes. If you like, serve extra basil and olive oil at the table so that everyone can add more to taste.

ZUPPA DI PEPERONI ARROSTI, CROSTINI DI MOZZARELLA E POMODORI SECCHI

ROASTED RED PEPPER SOUP WITH MOZZARELLA AND SUN-DRIED TOMATO CROSTINI

There is nothing quite like the taste of roasted red peppers and this vibrant soup, accompanied by delicious savoury crostini, is a treasure chest of flavours. Red peppers are amongst the richest vegetable sources of antioxidant vitamin C – one red pepper contains as much vitamin C as three oranges.

SERVES 4–6

8 large red peppers
4 tablespoons extra virgin olive oil
2 red onions, finely chopped
2 cloves garlic, finely chopped
1 fennel bulb, finely chopped
1 kg/2 lb ripe tomatoes, skinned, seeded and coarsely chopped
1 tablespoon balsamic vinegar
1 tablespoon caster sugar
600 ml/1 pint vegetable stock
freshly ground sea salt and black pepper
generous handful of basil leaves, coarsely torn
Mozzarella and Sun-dried Tomato Crostini
(see page 31), to serve

Preheat the oven to 180°C/350°F/Gas Mark 4. Roast the red peppers in the oven until the skins have blackened and blistered. Remove from the oven, place in a plastic bag and seal. When cool, peel off the skin, core and seed the peppers, then cut into thin strips.

Meanwhile, warm the olive oil in a large saucepan and add the red onion, garlic and fennel. Sweat the vegetables over a low heat for about 5 minutes, until soft and translucent but not coloured. Add the tomatoes and red peppers and cook over a very low heat for a further 5 minutes, to allow the flavours to develop. Stir in the vinegar and sugar, then add the stock, season with salt and pepper and simmer over a moderate heat for about 15 minutes.

Pour the soup into a food processor or blender and process until smooth. Strain into a clean saucepan and stir the basil leaves into the soup. Serve at once, accompanied by crostini.

ZUPPA DI FUNGHI PORCINI

WILD MUSHROOM SOUP

Italy's dense forests in the mountainous regions of Calabria are home to a wonderful variety of wild mushrooms, rich in potassium, and if you are fortunate enough to have your own local supply then you must try this sensational soup. If you are unable to find the fresh variety, use oyster mushrooms with 60g/2oz dried wild mushrooms.

SERVES 6

4 tablespoons extra virgin olive oil
4 shallots, finely chopped
2 cloves garlic, finely chopped
1 tablespoon tomato purée
1 kg/2 lb mixed wild mushrooms, coarsely chopped
1 litre/1¾ pints vegetable stock
2 tablespoons finely chopped fresh parsley
freshly ground sea salt and black pepper
90 g/3 oz finely grated Parmesan or Pecorino cheese

GARLIC BREAD CROUTES
6 thick slices of Olive Oil Bread (see page 244), crusts removed
extra virgin olive oil
2 cloves garlic, cut in half

Warm the olive oil in a large saucepan, then add the shallots and garlic. Cover and sweat over a low heat for about 5 minutes until soft and translucent, but not coloured. Stir in the tomato purée, then add the mushrooms and sauté for 3–4 minutes.

Pour in the stock, then simmer over a moderate heat for about 15 minutes. Remove from the heat, add the chopped parsley and season to taste with salt and pepper.

Meanwhile, prepare the croûtes. Preheat the oven to

180°C/350°F/Gas Mark 4. Brush the bread lightly all over with oil then place on a baking tray and bake for about 10 minutes, until lightly toasted. Rub the toasted bread all over with the cut sides of the garlic, so that it absorbs the flavour.

Place a slice of the garlic-scented bread in each soup bowl, then ladle the soup over the bread. Sprinkle with the grated Parmesan and serve piping hot.

BOUILLABAISSE

MEDITERRANEAN FISH SOUP

With such an abundance of wonderful fish and shellfish, it's hardly surprising that the Mediterranean is home to some of the finest fish soups, the most famous of which is bouillabaisse, a speciality of the port of Marseilles. Although a classic bouillabaisse is made with a large proportion of rascasse, a rock fish that is difficult to find outside the Mediterranean, there is no reason why we cannot savour the wonderful flavours and aromas of this divine fish soup using a selection of locally available fish.
A high dietary intake of fish is one of the key factors responsible for the low incidence of heart disease in the Mediterranean regions.

SERVES 8

125 ml/4 fl oz extra virgin olive oil
2 large onions, finely chopped
8 cloves garlic, finely chopped
1 leek, cut into fine julienne strips
1 fennel bulb, cut into fine julienne strips
1 kg/2 lb tomatoes, skinned, seeded and coarsely chopped
1 sprig of fresh thyme
2 bay leaves
zest of $^{1}/_{2}$ orange
freshly ground sea salt and black pepper
2.75 litres/$4^{1}/_{2}$ pints boiling water
1 teaspoon saffron threads
750 g/$1^{1}/_{2}$ lb fillet of red mullet, scaled, boned and cut into chunks
750 g/$1^{1}/_{2}$ lb fillet of sea bass, scaled, boned and cut into chunks
500 g/1 lb fillet of John Dory, scaled, boned and cut into chunks
250 g/8 oz monkfish tail, skinned and sliced

2 tablespoons Pernod
250 g/8 oz squid, cleaned and cut into rings, tentacles quartered
4 scallops, shelled and halved
8 large raw prawns, in their shells
16 mussels in their shells, scrubbed and beards removed

Warm 3 tablespoons of olive oil in a large casserole dish, then add the onions, garlic, leek and fennel. Sweat over a low heat for 4–5 minutes until soft and translucent, but not coloured. Add the tomatoes, thyme, bay leaves, orange zest and remaining olive oil, season with salt and pepper, then cook for another 4–5 minutes, until the tomatoes have softened to a pulp. Pour in the boiling water, increase the heat to high, then beat vigorously for about 2 minutes, so that the oil and water emulsifies. Boil vigorously for several minutes, beating from time to time, then reduce the heat and add the saffron threads.

Place the fish in the casserole, add the Pernod, then cover and poach for about 8 minutes. Add the squid, scallops, prawns and mussels to the casserole and simmer, covered, for a further 5 minutes.

Strain the soup through a colander and spoon the fish and vegetables into a large warm tureen, discarding any mussels that have failed to open. Return the stock to the saucepan and boil over a high heat until reduced by about one-third. Adjust the seasoning, then pour the hot stock over the fish and shellfish. Serve at once, with plenty of crusty bread.

BLACK OLIVE AND GARLIC CROSTINI

SERVES 4

175 g/6 oz good quality black olives, pitted
1 clove garlic, crushed
1 tablespoon capers, rinsed
2 anchovy fillets in olive oil, drained
1 teaspoon freshly squeezed lemon juice
4 tablespoons extra virgin olive oil
freshly ground black pepper
crusty bread such as French baguette or ciabatta, cut diagonally into 8 slices

Preheat the oven to 160°C/325°F/Gas Mark 3.

Place the black olives, garlic, capers, anchovy fillets and lemon juice in a food processor or blender and process until smooth. With the motor still running, add sufficient olive oil (about 2 tablespoons) to give a paste-like consistency. Season with plenty of black pepper.

Brush the bread lightly on both sides with the remaining olive oil, then bake in the preheated oven for 10–12 minutes, until golden brown. Leave the bread to cool, then spoon the black olive paste on top. Serve as an accompaniment to soup.

MOZZARELLA AND SUN-DRIED TOMATO CROSTINI

SERVES 4

4 sun-dried tomatoes in olive oil, coarsely chopped
1 tablespoon basil leaves, coarsely torn
½ clove garlic, chopped
90 ml/3 fl oz extra virgin olive oil
freshly ground black pepper
crusty bread such as French baguette or ciabatta, cut diagonally into 8 slices
8 small slices mozzarella cheese

Place the sun-dried tomatoes, basil leaves and garlic in a food processor and process for about 15 seconds. With the motor still running, add 1–2 tablespoons of olive oil, to moisten slightly. Do not over-process as the mixture should remain fairly coarse-textured. Season with pepper.

Brush the bread lightly on both sides with the remaining olive oil. Lightly toast one side of the bread under a medium grill, then turn over and place a slice of mozzarella on each crostini. Grill until the cheese has melted.

Spoon the tomato and basil mixture on to the melted cheese and serve as an accompaniment to soup.

RED PEPPER CROSTINI

SERVES 4

2 large red peppers
small handful of basil leaves, torn into small pieces
2 teaspoons chopped capers, rinsed
90 ml / 3 fl oz extra virgin olive oil
freshly ground sea salt and black pepper
crusty bread such as French baguette or ciabatta, cut diagonally
into 8 slices
2 cloves garlic, halved

Preheat the oven to 180°C/350°F/Gas Mark 4. Roast the red peppers in the preheated oven for about 15 minutes, until the skins have blackened and blistered. Remove from the oven, place in a plastic bag and seal. When cool, peel off the skin and core and seed the peppers. Dice the flesh then add the basil leaves and capers. Drizzle with a little olive oil to moisten, then season to taste with salt and pepper.

Reduce the oven temperature to 160°C/325°F/Gas Mark 3. Brush the bread lightly on both sides with olive oil and bake in the preheated oven for 10–12 minutes, until golden brown.

Rub one side of the toasted bread with the cut side of the garlic cloves, so that it is flavoured with a hint of garlic. Spoon the red peppers on to the crostini and serve as an accompaniment to soup.

TUNA CANAPES

SERVES 4

½ French baguette, cut into 8 rounds
extra virgin olive oil
175 g/6 oz tuna in olive oil, drained
1 tablespoon finely chopped onion
1 tablespoon finely chopped fresh parsley
freshly ground black pepper

Preheat the oven to 160°C/325°F/Gas Mark 3.

Brush the bread slices lightly on both sides with olive oil. Bake in the preheated oven for 10–12 minutes, until golden brown.

Flake the tuna lightly with a fork and mix in the chopped onion and parsley. Season with plenty of black pepper. Spoon the tuna on to the baked canapés and serve as an accompaniment to soup.

PROVENCAL CROUSTADES

SERVES 4

1 tablespoon capers, rinsed
125 g/4 oz pitted black olives
4 anchovy fillets in olive oil, drained
60 g/2 oz tuna in olive oil, drained
1 clove garlic, coarsely chopped
1 tablespoon freshly squeezed lemon juice
90 ml/3 fl oz extra virgin olive oil
freshly ground black pepper
$1/2$ French baguette, cut into 8 rounds
2 hard-boiled eggs, each sliced in 4
1 tablespoon finely chopped parsley

Preheat the oven to 160°C/325°F/Gas Mark 3.

Place the capers, olives, anchovies, tuna and garlic in a food processor or blender and process until smooth. With the motor still running, add the lemon juice and sufficient olive oil to give a paste-like consistency (about 2–3 tablespoons). Season with plenty of black pepper.

Brush the bread slices lightly on both sides with the remaining olive oil. Bake in the preheated oven for 10–12 minutes, until golden brown.

Spoon the olive and anchovy mixture on to the baked croustades, then top with a slice of hard-boiled egg. Sprinkle with parsley and serve as an accompaniment to soup.

GARLIC CROUTONS

1 clove garlic, crushed
90 ml/3 fl oz extra virgin olive oil
4 slices day-old Olive Oil Bread (see page 244), crusts removed
and cut into 1 cm/¹/₂ inch squares.

Place the garlic and olive oil in a screw-topped jar and shake well. Leave for about 30 minutes, so that the olive oil is strongly perfumed with the garlic.

Preheat the oven to 160°C/325°F/Gas Mark 3.

Place the bread squares in a bowl and strain on the garlic-scented oil. Toss well so that the bread absorbs all the oil. Spread out the bread squares in an ovenproof dish and bake in the preheated oven for about 10 minutes, until golden. Serve the croûtons as an accompaniment to soups and salads.

BASIL CROUTONS

generous handful of fresh basil leaves
90 ml/3 fl oz extra virgin olive oil
4 slices day-old Olive Oil Bread (see page 244), crusts removed
and cut into 1 cm/¹/₂ inch squares

Preheat the oven to 160°C/325°F/Gas Mark 3.

Place the basil leaves and olive oil in a food processor or blender and process until smooth.

Place the bread squares in a bowl and pour on the basil oil. Toss well so that the bread absorbs all the oil. Spread out the bread squares in an ovenproof baking dish and bake in the preheated oven for about 10 minutes, until crisp. Basil croûtons make a particularly good accompaniment to tomato-based soups.

2
Salads

SALATA KRITIKI

CRETAN-STYLE ORANGE AND WATERCRESS SALAD

This light, refreshing salad combines the peppery flavour of watercress with sweet oranges, plump black olives, melt-in-the-mouth feta cheese and a wonderful vinaigrette flavoured with a hint of raspberry.
Watercress leaves are highly nutritious, containing large amounts of the powerful antioxidant vitamin beta-carotene, as well as the minerals iron and calcium.

SERVES 4

4 large oranges, peeled and divided into segments, pith and membrane removed
1 large bunch of watercress, divided into sprigs
90 g / 3 oz black olives
125 g / 4 oz feta cheese, cubed

DRESSING
100 ml / 3½ fl oz extra virgin olive oil
2 tablespoons raspberry vinegar
½ teaspoon Dijon mustard
½ teaspoon clear honey
freshly ground sea salt and black pepper

To make the dressing, whisk the olive oil and raspberry vinegar together until thoroughly emulsified. Add the Dijon mustard and honey and blend well together. Season with salt and pepper.

Arrange the orange segments, watercress and black olives on individual serving plates, then drizzle with the raspberry-scented dressing. Arrange the feta cheese over the salad and serve immediately.

INSALATA DI FEGATINI

WARM SALAD OF CHICKEN LIVERS

Chicken livers are very popular in Italy and often appear in pasta sauces, or with rice, and most delicious of all, I think, in this wonderful warm salad, combining healthy salad leaves with a good balance of other nutrients.

SERVES 4

250 g/8 oz chicken livers
4 tablespoons extra virgin olive oil
handful of pink radicchio leaves
handful of green frisée
handful of rocket leaves
4 tablespoons Garlic Croûtons (see page 35)
4 oranges, peeled and cut into segments, pith and membrane removed

WALNUT-SCENTED DRESSING
125 ml/4 fl oz extra virgin olive oil
90 ml/3 fl oz walnut oil
2 tablespoons red wine vinegar
½ teaspoon Dijon mustard
2 teaspoons freshly squeezed lemon juice
½ teaspoon sugar
freshly ground sea salt and black pepper

Soak the chicken livers in cold water for 10 minutes, changing the water once during the soaking time. Just before cooking, drain the chicken livers and pat dry.

Prepare the dressing by whisking the olive oil, walnut oil and vinegar together, until it has emulsified. Add the Dijon mustard, lemon juice and sugar, mixing well. Season to taste with salt and pepper.

Warm the olive oil in a large frying pan, then add the chicken livers. Sauté over a moderate heat for 4–5 minutes, turning the livers from time to time so that they are evenly cooked. Remove the livers with a slotted spoon and keep warm. Pour off all but 1 tablespoon of the oil, then pour in the dressing. Stir to deglaze the pan over a moderate heat, so that the dressing is just gently warmed.

Mix the salad leaves in a bowl, then strain on the warm dressing and toss well. Place the salad leaves on individual serving plates, then arrange the warm chicken livers and garlic croûtons on top. Arrange the orange segments decoratively over the salad and serve at once.

HORIATIKI SALATA

GREEK COUNTRY SALAD

This simple country salad is a popular dish in tavernas throughout Greece. The four essential ingredients are tomatoes, cucumber, feta cheese and olives, all excellent sources of vitamins and minerals. Other ingredients such as capers, red onion, green pepper and rocket leaves are often added according to taste.

SERVES 4

6 ripe but firm tomatoes, cut into quarters
1/2 cucumber, halved lengthways, then finely sliced
1 red onion, sliced thinly into rings
1 green pepper, cored, seeded and sliced thinly into rings
1 tablespoon small capers, drained
100 ml / 3 1/2 fl oz extra virgin olive oil
1 tablespoon freshly squeezed lemon juice
freshly ground sea salt and black pepper
generous handful of rocket leaves
125 g / 4 oz feta cheese, cut into small pieces
16 black olives, pitted
2 tablespoons finely chopped parsley

Mix the tomatoes, cucumber, red onion, green pepper and capers in a bowl. Whisk the olive oil and lemon juice together until thoroughly emulsified, and season to taste with salt and pepper. Drizzle the lemon and oil dressing over the salad and toss well.

Arrange the rocket leaves on a serving platter, then spoon the dressed salad on to the leaves. Arrange the feta cheese and black olives decoratively over the salad and sprinkle with chopped fresh parsley.

INSALATA TRICOLORE

TOMATO, MOZZARELLA AND BASIL SALAD

This trio of Italian colours and flavours make perfect partners and are wonderful together in this simple salad. Used so extensively in Italian cuisine, both tomatoes and olive oil are brimming with healthy nutrients.

SERVES 4

8 large Mediterranean tomatoes, cut into thick slices
250 g/8 oz mozzarella cheese, cut into thick slices
2 generous handfuls of basil leaves, coarsely torn
freshly ground sea salt and black pepper
extra virgin olive oil

Lay alternate slices of tomato and mozzarella on individual plates, forming circles. Scatter the basil leaves over the salad. Season with salt and pepper, then drizzle the olive oil liberally all over the salad. Serve at once.

ENSALADA DE SARDINAS DE LA SIERRA

SALAD OF FRESH SARDINES

I first tasted this wonderful Spanish salad in a tiny restaurant nesting in the foothills of the Sierra Nevada, overlooking the enchanting town of Granada. The flavours marry beautifully together. The fresh sardines are stuffed with roasted red peppers, then oven-baked with lemon and parsley and served warm on a bed of fresh green salad leaves. A sherry-scented tomato vinaigrette makes the perfect dressing.
Sardines are one of the most important sources of omega-3 essential fatty acids, nutrients that are closely linked with the Mediterranean's low rate of heart disease.

SERVES 4

3 large red peppers
12 medium-sized sardines, scaled and boned, heads and tails removed
freshly squeezed juice of 1 lemon, strained
4 tablespoons extra virgin olive oil
125 ml/4 fl oz dry white wine
2 cloves garlic, finely chopped
2 tablespoons finely chopped parsley
4 generous handfuls of mixed green salad leaves

TOMATO VINAIGRETTE
150 ml/^{1}/$_4$ pint extra virgin olive oil
2 tablespoons sherry vinegar
^{1}/$_2$ teaspoon Dijon mustard
^{1}/$_2$ teaspoon brown sugar
3 large tomatoes, skinned, seeded and finely chopped
freshly ground sea salt and black pepper

Preheat the oven to 180°C/350°F/Gas Mark 4. Roast the peppers in the preheated oven until their skins have blackened and blistered. Place in a plastic bag, seal and leave to cool. When cool, peel off the skin, core and seed the peppers, then cut into strips. Stuff each sardine with a strip of red pepper, and reserve the rest for garnish. Arrange the sardines in a large ovenproof dish.

Increase the oven temperature to 190°C/375°F/Gas Mark 5. Mix together the lemon juice, olive oil, white wine, garlic and parsley, then pour over the sardines. Bake in the preheated oven for 15–20 minutes, basting from time to time. Remove from the oven and allow to cool a little in the cooking juices.

To make the vinaigrette, whisk the olive oil and vinegar together until thoroughly emulsified. Stir in the mustard and sugar, then add the finely chopped tomatoes. Season with salt and pepper.

To serve, arrange the salad leaves on 4 individual serving plates. Lay the baked sardines, still lukewarm, over the salad leaves and garnish with the remaining strips of red pepper. Drizzle the tomato vinaigrette over the salad and serve at once.

SALADE DE LENTILLES AU FENOUIL

SALAD OF PUY LENTILS WITH FENNEL

Lentils are highly nutritious and the green lentil from the
Le Puy region of France is the most flavoursome of all. In
this delicious salad, the earthy flavour of the lentils marries
well with the strong aniseed flavour of the fennel.

SERVES 4

250 g/8 oz Puy lentils
1 large onion, quartered
2 cloves garlic, finely chopped
1 bouquet garni
125 ml/4 fl oz extra virgin olive oil
2 tablespoons balsamic vinegar
1 fennel bulb, cut into fine julienne strips, feathery leaves reserved
3 tomatoes, skinned, seeded and finely chopped
2 shallots, finely chopped
freshly ground sea salt and black pepper
1 tablespoon chopped chives

Rinse the lentils, discarding any discoloured ones. Place in a
large saucepan, cover with water, then add the onion, garlic
and bouquet garni. Simmer over a moderate heat for about
25–30 minutes, until tender but not mushy.

Drain the lentils immediately, discarding the onion and
bouquet garni. Whisk the olive oil and vinegar together
until thoroughly emulsified, then pour the dressing over the
lentils while still warm and toss well.

Mix the fennel strips, tomatoes and shallots into the
lentils and season to taste with salt and pepper.

Finely chop the reserved fennel leaves and combine with
the chopped chives. Sprinkle over the salad, which is equally
delicious served lukewarm or cold.

INSALATA DI PEPERONI ALLA NAPOLETANA

ROASTED RED AND YELLOW PEPPER SALAD WITH ANCHOVIES, CAPERS AND GARLIC

Roasting or grilling peppers brings out their wonderful sweet flavour. Both red and yellow peppers are a rich source of vitamin C and provide valuable amounts of antioxidant beta-carotene. Here they are served quite simply with anchovies, capers, garlic and basil, with a generous helping of extra virgin olive oil, a healthy monounsaturated fat.

SERVES 4

4 large red peppers
4 large yellow peppers
2 tablespoons small capers, drained
125 g/4 oz anchovies in olive oil, drained
2 cloves garlic, cut into fine slivers
generous handful of basil leaves, coarsely torn
125 ml/4 fl oz extra virgin olive oil

Preheat the oven to 180°F/350°C/Gas Mark 4. Roast the peppers in the preheated oven until the skins have blackened and blistered. Place in a plastic bag, seal and leave to cool. When cool, peel off the skin, core and seed the peppers and cut into strips.

Arrange the peppers on a serving platter, alternating the red and yellow strips. Arrange the capers, anchovies and garlic over the peppers, then sprinkle with the basil leaves. Drizzle a generous amount of olive oil over the salad before serving.

INSALATA DI FINOCCHIO ALLA GRIGLIA CON POMODORE E SPINACI

SALAD OF GRILLED FENNEL WITH TOMATOES AND WILTED SPINACH

Grilled fennel has a wonderfully intense, aromatic flavour that marries really well with tomatoes and spinach. Fennel is very low in calories, contains useful amounts of beta-carotene and is rich in potassium. Spinach is one of the most nutritious vegetables you can eat.

SERVES 4

2 fennel bulbs cut lengthways into 6 pieces, feathery leaves reserved
2 tablespoons extra virgin olive oil
350 g / 12 oz baby spinach leaves, stalks removed, rinsed and drained
freshly ground sea salt and black pepper

DRESSING
150 ml / 1/4 pint extra virgin olive oil
2 tablespoons balsamic vinegar
1 clove garlic, crushed
4 tomatoes, skinned, seeded and finely chopped
handful of basil leaves, coarsely torn

Brush the fennel pieces with olive oil. Place under a hot grill and grill for about 2 minutes on each side until lightly charred and just tender, but still firm.

Finely chop the reserved fennel leaves. Place the spinach and 1 tablespoon of the fennel leaves in a saucepan and season with salt and pepper. Allow to wilt over a moderate heat for 2–3 minutes. To make the dressing, whisk the olive oil and vinegar together until thoroughly emulsified. Stir in the garlic, tomatoes and basil leaves and season to taste.

To serve, place the wilted spinach leaves in the centre of 4 individual serving plates, then arrange the grilled fennel on top. Spoon the vinaigrette in a circle around the spinach, drizzling some over the fennel as well. Serve at once while still warm.

SALADE DE CRABE AUX AGRUMES ET AU VINAIGRE DE CHAMPAGNE

SALAD OF CRAB WITH CITRUS FRUITS AND CHAMPAGNE VINAIGRETTE

Citrus fruits are partnered with fresh crab meat in this simple salad, dressed with a sparkling vinaigrette.

SERVES 4

350 g / 12 oz white crab meat
2 shallots, finely chopped
½ fennel bulb, finely chopped
2 tomatoes, skinned, seeded and finely chopped
4 generous handfuls of rocket leaves
4 oranges, peeled and cut into segments, pith and membrane removed
2 pink grapefruit, peeled and cut into segments, pith and membrane removed

CHAMPAGNE VINAIGRETTE
125 ml / 4 fl oz extra virgin olive oil
2 tablespoons champagne vinegar
½ teaspoon Dijon mustard
½ teaspoon brown sugar
freshly ground sea salt and black pepper

Flake the crab meat into small pieces, then mix with the shallots, fennel and tomatoes. Place the rocket leaves in the centre of 4 plates and arrange the orange and grapefruit segments around the rocket. Spoon the crab salad over the rocket.

To make the vinaigrette, whisk the olive oil and vinegar together until thoroughly emulsified. Add the Dijon mustard and brown sugar, mix well and season with salt and pepper. Drizzle the vinaigrette over the crab salad.

SALADE DE COQUILLES SAINT JACQUES AU FENOUIL

WARM SALAD OF SEARED SCALLOPS WITH FENNEL

This is one of those beautiful warm salads that takes only minutes to prepare, yet is bursting with the wonderfully intense aromas of the South of France.

SERVES 4

2 fennel bulbs, stalk included, sliced lengthways
200 ml/7 fl oz extra virgin olive oil
12 scallops, shelled
freshly ground sea salt and black pepper
90 ml/3 fl oz dry white vermouth
freshly squeezed juice of ½ lemon
1 clove garlic, crushed
2 tablespoons finely chopped chervil
4 handfuls of mixed green salad leaves

Brush the fennel lightly with olive oil, then cook under a moderate grill for about 3 minutes until lightly charred, but still crisp and firm.

Pat the scallops dry and season lightly. Heat 3 tablespoons of olive oil in a frying pan, then quickly sauté the scallops for 1 minute only on each side, so that they remain moist. Remove from the pan with a slotted spoon, then pour in the vermouth and stir until it has nearly all evaporated.

Add the remaining olive oil, lemon juice and garlic to the pan and warm very gently for about 1 minute, then remove from the heat and add the chervil.

To serve, place the grilled fennel on individual serving plates, then arrange mixed salad leaves over the fennel. Arrange the seared scallops on the salad leaves, then drizzle on the chervil dressing. Serve at once while still lukewarm.

INSALATA DI GAMBERETTI ALLA GRIGLIA

SALAD OF GRILLED MEDITERRANEAN PRAWNS
WITH SUN-DRIED TOMATO VINAIGRETTE

Grilled prawns are one of life's simple pleasures, particularly
when served with crisp green salad leaves and this divine
sun-dried tomato vinaigrette.
Extremely low in saturated fat, prawns are an excellent
source of protein, vitamin B12 and selenium.

SERVES 4

16 large raw prawns, shelled with tails left on
freshly ground sea salt and black pepper
2 tablespoons extra virgin olive oil
1 large red pepper, cored, seeded and cut into 12 pieces
4 generous handfuls of mixed green salad leaves

SUN-DRIED TOMATO VINAIGRETTE
125 g/4 oz sun-dried tomatoes in olive oil, drained and coarsely
chopped
175 ml/6 fl oz extra virgin olive oil
2 tablespoons balsamic vinegar
1 clove garlic, coarsely chopped
handful of basil leaves, torn into small pieces

Carefully make an incision down the back of the prawns
and remove the dark intestinal vein. Season the prawns with
black pepper, then brush lightly with olive oil.

Thread the prawns and red pepper pieces on skewers,
then place under a hot grill. Grill for 1½–2 minutes on each
side, turning once.

To make the vinaigrette, place the tomatoes, olive oil,
vinegar and garlic in a food processor or blender and process

for about 1 minute. Season to taste with salt and pepper, then stir in the basil leaves.

To serve, arrange the salad leaves on individual serving plates, then lay the prawn and pepper skewers on top. Spoon the vinaigrette around the salad. The vinaigrette will separate on the plate, creating a red and green mosaic pattern.

ESCALIVADA

SALAD OF GRILLED MEDITERRANEAN VEGETABLES WITH TOMATO AND BASIL VINAIGRETTE

Escalivada is a speciality of the Catalan region of Spain. Strictly speaking, it is made only with peppers, aubergine and onions, drizzled with olive oil, but I like to add courgettes and artichoke, and serve it with a tomato and basil vinaigrette. The vegetables may be either grilled or roasted, and served lukewarm or cold, according to taste. Substantial amounts of vitamins and minerals are provided by the vegetables in this dish.

SERVES 4

2 red peppers
1 yellow pepper
1 large aubergine, cut into 1 cm / $^1/_2$ inch slices
1 large courgette, cut into 1 cm / $^1/_2$ inch slices
1 large red onion, cut into 8 wedges
1 artichoke, trimmed and cut into 8 wedges
extra virgin olive oil
freshly ground sea salt and black pepper
4 handfuls of mixed salad leaves

TOMATO AND BASIL VINAIGRETTE
175 ml / 6 fl oz extra virgin olive oil
1 tablespoon balsamic vinegar
1 tablespoon freshly squeezed lemon juice
$^1/_2$ teaspoon Dijon mustard
$^1/_2$ teaspoon brown sugar
3 large tomatoes, skinned, seeded and finely chopped
1 clove garlic, crushed
handful of basil leaves

Grill the peppers under a hot grill until the skins have blackened and blistered. Place in a plastic bag, seal and leave to cool. Peel off the skin, core and seed the peppers, and cut lengthways into thin slices.

Brush the remaining vegetables lightly with olive oil and season with salt and pepper. Place in a grill pan and grill for 2–3 minutes on each side, turning once. The vegetables should be golden brown and just tender.

To make the vinaigrette, blend the olive oil, balsamic vinegar and lemon juice together until emulsified. Mix in the Dijon mustard and brown sugar. Add the tomatoes to the vinaigrette, together with the garlic and basil, and season with salt and pepper. To serve, place some salad leaves in the centre of individual serving plates, then arrange the grilled vegetables on top. Drizzle the vinaigrette over the vegetables and serve at once, while still warm.

KALAMARI SALATA

SALAD OF SQUID WITH THREE HERB DRESSING

Three aromatic herbs are used to flavour this beautiful salad from the Greek islands. Squid is an excellent source of the important antioxidant trace mineral, selenium.

SERVES 4–6

150 ml / ¼ pint fish stock
150 ml / ¼ pint dry white wine
2 shallots, finely chopped
1 clove garlic, finely chopped
500 g / 1 lb squid, cleaned and cut into rings, tentacles reserved
3 ripe tomatoes, chopped into small pieces
1 fennel bulb, cut into fine julienne strips
sprigs of chervil, to garnish

THREE HERB DRESSING
175 ml / 6 fl oz extra virgin olive oil
freshly squeezed juice of 1 lemon
½ teaspoon Dijon mustard
1 tablespoon finely chopped flat-leaf parsley
1 tablespoon finely chopped chervil
1 tablespoon finely chopped basil leaves
freshly ground sea salt and black pepper

Place the fish stock, white wine, shallots, garlic and squid tentacles in a saucepan and bring to the boil. Boil for about 1 minute, then reduce the heat to medium and add the squid rings. Poach over a moderate heat for 6–8 minutes, until the squid is tender but still firm. Remove the squid from the saucepan with a slotted spoon and set aside. Boil the stock over a high heat until reduced to about 2 tablespoons.

Meanwhile, to make the dressing, whisk the olive oil,

lemon juice and Dijon mustard together until thoroughly emulsified. Add the reduced fish stock and the fresh herbs, then season to taste with salt and pepper.

Mix the squid, tomatoes and fennel together, then pour over the dressing, tossing well. Serve on a large platter, garnished with sprigs of chervil.

SALADE DE ROQUETTE ET TOMATES AUX PIGNONS

SALAD OF ROCKET AND MEDITERRANEAN TOMATOES WITH PINE NUTS

Vibrant Mediterranean flavours and colours are contained in this simple salad. Both rocket leaves and tomatoes provide a high concentration of carotenoid nutrients, while pine nuts and olives are rich sources of vitamin E.

SERVES 4

6 large Mediterranean tomatoes, sliced
125 g/4 oz rocket leaves
60 g/2 oz black olives
3 tablespoons pine nuts
60 g/2 oz Parmesan cheese, cut into fine shavings
2 tablespoons warm Garlic Croûtons (see page 35)

BASIL AND WALNUT VINAIGRETTE
4 tablespoons extra virgin olive oil
2 tablespoons walnut oil
2 tablespoons freshly squeezed lemon juice
1/2 teaspoon Dijon mustard
1/2 teaspoon clear honey
generous handful of fresh basil leaves, coarsely torn
freshly ground sea salt and black pepper

Place the tomatoes in a large salad bowl with the rocket leaves and black olives.

Place the pine nuts in a dry, heavy-based saucepan over moderate heat for about 3 minutes, until they turn golden brown. Remove from the heat and allow to cool, then add to the salad.

To make the vinaigrette, whisk the olive oil, walnut oil

and lemon juice together until thoroughly emulsified. Add the Dijon mustard, honey and fresh basil, mixing well. Season with salt and pepper.

Pour the vinaigrette over the salad and toss well. Sprinkle the Parmesan shavings and garlic croûtons over the salad and serve at once.

INSALATA DI FRUTTI DI MARE ALLA GRIGLIA

GRILLED SEAFOOD SALAD

Seafood salad appears on the menu of almost every Italian restaurant, and as a result there are many variations. The three most important ingredients are mussels, squid and prawns, with other seafood such as scallops, clams, oysters or octopus added according to preference and availability. Rich in vitamins and minerals, seafood is a highly nutritious, low-fat source of protein.

SERVES 6

750 g / 1½ lb mussels in their shells, scrubbed and beards removed
125 ml / 4 fl oz dry white wine
1 shallot, finely chopped
1 clove garlic, crushed
500 g / 1 lb raw prawns, shelled and deveined
500 g / 1 lb squid, cleaned, cut into rings and tentacles halved
12 queen scallops, shelled
mixed salad leaves
lemon wedges, to garnish

LEMON AND HERB VINAIGRETTE
175 ml / 6 fl oz extra virgin olive oil
freshly squeezed juice of 1 lemon
½ teaspoon Dijon mustard
1 clove garlic, crushed
1 tablespoon finely chopped flat-leaf parsley
1 tablespoon finely chopped chervil
freshly ground sea salt and black pepper

Discard any mussel shells that are not tightly closed. Place the white wine, shallot and garlic in a large saucepan and bring to the boil. Add the mussels, cover and boil over a fairly high heat for several minutes, until all the shells have opened. Strain the musssels and shell them, reserving the juices and the cooking liquid. Discard any mussels that have failed to open. Boil the juices and cooking liquid over a high heat, until reduced to 1 tablespoon.

Lay the prawns, squid and scallops on a lightly oiled grill pan and cook briefly under a very hot grill, allowing 1 minute each side for the squid rings and prawns, and 30 seconds each side for the scallops. The squid tentacles will need about 1½ minutes each side. To prepare the dressing, whisk the olive oil, lemon juice and Dijon mustard together until emulsified. Add the reduced mussel juices, the garlic and the herbs, mixing well. Season to taste with salt and pepper.

Place the mixed salad leaves on a large serving platter, then arrange the mussels, squid, prawns and scallops on top. Spoon over the dressing, garnish with lemon wedges and serve at once, while the seafood is still warm.

INSALATA DI FUNGHI

WARM SALAD OF BALSAMIC-SCENTED MUSHROOMS WITH PARMESAN TUILES

Fresh mushrooms always make a simple yet very appealing salad. Certain varieties may have the same blood-thinning characteristics as those attributed to garlic and onion. It is believed that some varieties of wild mushrooms may also help to stimulate the immune system.

SERVES 4

4 generous handfuls of mixed salad leaves, including rocket,
radicchio and frisée
175 ml / 6 fl oz extra virgin olive oil
500 g / 1 lb mixed mushrooms, such as oyster, shiitake,
chanterelles or ceps
2 cloves garlic, crushed
3 tablespoons finely chopped parsley
2 tablespoons balsamic vinegar

PARMESAN TUILES
125 g / 4 oz finely grated Parmesan cheese
1½ teaspoons plain flour

Make the Parmesan tuiles first. Preheat the oven to 180°C/ 350°F/Gas Mark 4. Line 2 large baking trays with non-stick baking parchment and oil lightly. Mix the grated Parmesan and the flour together. Spoon level tablespoons of the cheese mixture on the baking trays, forming circles. Space the circles about 10cm/4 inches apart, allowing room for the tuiles to spread. Bake in the preheated oven for 8–10 minutes, until golden. Allow to cool, then carefully remove the tuiles from the baking tray, using a spatula. Arrange the salad leaves on individual serving plates.

Warm half the olive oil in a large frying pan, then add the

mushrooms and garlic. Sauté over a moderate heat for 3–4 minutes, until the mushrooms are tender, but not too soft. Stir in the fresh parsley. Using a slotted spoon, remove the mushrooms from the pan and arrange on top of the salad leaves.

Add the remaining olive oil and the balsamic vinegar to the pan and warm over a very low heat, so that the dressing is just lukewarm, then drizzle over and around the mushrooms and salad leaves. Arrange one Parmesan tuile on each plate and serve at once, while still warm.

INSALATA DI BROCCOLI

SALAD OF BROCCOLI WITH BLACK OLIVES AND ROASTED RED PEPPER VINAIGRETTE

A vibrant roasted red pepper vinaigrette makes a delicious accompaniment to these broccoli florets, steamed until just al dente. Broccoli is rich in a number of compounds believed to work as powerful anti-cancer agents. It also contains high levels of antioxidant carotenoid nutrients, and is a rich source of selenium, a trace mineral that plays a key part in maintaining a healthy immune system.

SERVES 4

1 kg/2 lb broccoli, divided into large florets
16 black olives, pitted
75 g/2½ oz pine nuts, lightly toasted
1 tablespoon capers, drained
handful of basil leaves
8 anchovy fillets in olive oil, drained

ROASTED RED PEPPER VINAIGRETTE
2 large red peppers
175 ml/6 fl oz extra virgin olive oil
2 tablespoons balsamic vinegar
½ teaspoon Dijon mustard
½ teaspoon brown sugar
freshly ground sea salt and black pepper

Preheat the oven to 180°C/ 350°F/Gas Mark 4.

Steam the broccoli over lightly salted boiling water for about 2 minutes, until tender but still firm and crunchy. Refresh immediately under cold running water, then drain well. Place the broccoli florets in a salad bowl and add the black olives, pine nuts and capers.

Roast the red peppers in the preheated oven for about 15

minutes, until the skins have blackened and blistered. Place the roasted peppers in a plastic bag, seal and leave to cool. When cool, peel off the skin, core and seed the peppers then cut into fine dice.

Whisk the olive oil and vinegar together until thoroughly emulsified, then add the Dijon mustard and sugar, mixing well. Add the diced red pepper. Spoon the vinaigrette over the broccoli and toss carefully. Sprinkle the basil leaves over the salad, then garnish with the anchovy fillets.

SALADE NICOISE

SALAD OF MIXED MEDITERRANEAN VEGETABLES WITH FRESH TUNA

This colourful Mediterranean mixture of tuna, French beans, eggs, tomatoes, potatoes, anchovies and olives, nesting on a bed of salad leaves, makes a heavenly combination. Much more than just a simple salad, this is a well balanced meal in itself, packed with important health-protecting nutrients. Most of the essential oils are removed from the tuna before it is canned, so use fresh tuna whenever possible.

SERVES 4

4 generous handfuls of mixed salad leaves, including rocket, radicchio and frisée
4 soft-boiled eggs, shelled and quartered
175 g/6 oz baby new potatoes, boiled and sliced
125 g/4 oz green beans, steamed but still crisp
8 small tomatoes, cut into quarters
3 tablespoons extra virgin olive oil
4 x 100 g/3½ oz fresh tuna fillets
8 anchovy fillets in olive oil, drained
90 g/3 oz black olives, to garnish

NIÇOISE DRESSING
175 ml/6 fl oz extra virgin olive oil
2 tablespoons red wine vinegar
½ teaspoon Dijon mustard
½ teaspoon brown sugar
1 clove garlic, crushed
generous handful of basil leaves, torn into small pieces
freshly ground sea salt and black pepper

Place the salad leaves on individual serving plates, then arrange the soft-boiled eggs, potatoes, green beans and tomatoes decoratively over the mixed leaves.

Heat the olive oil in a frying pan and sear the tuna over a moderately high heat for about 2 minutes on each side, so that the fish remains slightly pink and moist inside. Remove the tuna fillets with a slotted spoon and place one on each plate.

To make the dressing, warm the olive oil over a very low heat, then remove from the heat and add the vinegar, Dijon mustard and sugar, mixing well until thoroughly emulsified. Add the garlic and basil leaves, and season with salt and pepper. Pour the warm oil over the tuna and salad, then garnish with the anchovies and black olives.

Serve at once, while the tuna is still lukewarm.

SALADE DE COUSCOUS AUX FRUITS DE MER

SALAD OF COUSCOUS WITH SHELLFISH

A staple North African food, couscous is a popular accompaniment to chicken, fish and meat dishes in both Morocco and Tunisia. Derived from durum wheat, couscous is a valuable source of complex carbohydrates.

SERVES 4

250 g/8 oz pre-cooked couscous
175 ml/6 fl oz hot vegetable stock
4 tomatoes, skinned, seeded and finely chopped
1 red onion, finely chopped
1 red pepper, cored, seeded and finely chopped
3 cloves garlic, crushed
generous handful of rocket leaves, coarsely chopped
2 tablespoons coarsely chopped flat-leaf parsley
8 large prawns in their shells

VINAIGRETTE
4 tablespoons extra virgin olive oil
2 tablespoons walnut oil
2 tablespoons balsamic vinegar
$1/2$ teaspoon Dijon mustard
$1/2$ teaspoon brown sugar
$1/2$ red chilli pepper, seeded and finely chopped
freshly ground sea salt and black pepper

Place the couscous in a shallow bowl and cover with the hot vegetable stock. Leave to swell for about 15 minutes, absorbing all the liquid, then transfer to a large salad bowl and leave to dry out for about an hour, fluffing up with a fork to separate the grains.

To make the vinaigrette, whisk the olive oil, walnut oil and   vinegar together until thoroughly emulsified, then add the Dijon mustard, sugar and chilli pepper, mixing well. Season with salt and pepper.

Add the tomatoes, onion, pepper, garlic, rocket leaves and parsley to the couscous, then pour over the vinaigrette, tossing well. Arrange the prawns over the salad to garnish and serve.

INSALATA DI FAGIOLI ALLA TOSCANA

TUSCAN BEAN SALAD WITH TRIO OF RED VEGETABLES

Red onion, peppers and tomatoes add vibrant colours and flavours to this salad of Italian cannellini beans, dressed with a garlic and herb vinaigrette. Pulses are enjoyed extensively in the Mediterranean, providing valuable amounts of protein, B vitamins, iron and fibre.

SERVES 4

250 g/8 oz cannellini beans, soaked overnight with 2 tablespoons bicarbonate of soda
2 red peppers, halved, cored and seeded
125 g/4 oz green beans, cut into 2.5 cm/1 inch pieces
250 g/8 oz tomatoes, skinned, seeded and finely chopped
1 red onion, finely chopped

GARLIC AND HERB VINAIGRETTE
125 ml/4 fl oz extra virgin olive oil
3 tablespoons walnut oil
2 tablespoons red wine vinegar
½ teaspoon Dijon mustard
½ teaspoon brown sugar
1 clove garlic, crushed
1 tablespoon finely chopped parsley
generous handful of basil leaves, coarsely torn
freshly ground sea salt and black pepper

Drain the beans and rinse well. Place in a clean saucepan and cover with cold water. Bring to the boil, then simmer over a moderate heat for about 1 hour, until just tender, but not too soggy or falling apart.

Grill the red peppers under a medium heat until the skins have blackened and blistered. Place in a plastic bag, seal and leave to cool. Peel off the skins, core and seed the peppers then cut into 1 cm/½ inch squares.

Steam the green beans over lightly salted boiling water until just tender, but still al dente.

To prepare the vinaigrette, whisk the olive oil, walnut oil and vinegar together until thoroughly emulsified, then add the Dijon mustard and sugar, mixing well. Add the garlic and herbs and season with salt and pepper.

Drain the beans well and transfer to a large serving bowl. Pour the garlic and herb vinaigrette over the beans while still warm and toss well. Add the red peppers, green beans, tomatoes and red onion to the beans and toss well. Serve the salad at room temperature.

ENSALADA DE PIPERRADA

SALAD OF TOMATOES, SWEET PEPPERS AND QUAIL'S EGGS WITH WALNUT VINAIGRETTE

This salad is a hot-weather version of the famous Basque *piperrada*, a hot dish of scrambled eggs, tomatoes, peppers and onions.

SERVES 4

500 g/1 lb tomatoes, sliced
1 red onion, finely sliced
1 clove garlic, crushed
1 large red and 1 large green pepper, cored, seeded and cut lengthways into strips
½ cucumber, finely sliced
20 black olives, pitted
125 g/4 oz baby spinach leaves, rinsed and dried, stalks removed
2 tablespoons coarsely chopped flat-leaf parsley
4 quails' eggs, soft-boiled, shelled and halved

WALNUT VINAIGRETTE
4 tablespoons extra virgin olive oil
2 tablespoons walnut oil
2 tablespoons sherry vinegar
1 teaspoon wholegrain mustard
½ teaspoon brown sugar
freshly ground sea salt and black pepper

Combine the tomatoes, red onion, garlic, peppers, cucumber, olives, spinach leaves and parsley in a large salad bowl.

To make the vinaigrette, whisk the oils and vinegar together until thoroughly emulsified. Add the mustard and sugar, mixing well, then season. Pour over the salad and toss well. Garnish with the quails' eggs.

3
Starters and Light Meals

MEJILLONES A LA MARINERA

MUSSELS COOKED FISHERMAN'S STYLE, WITH WHITE WINE, GARLIC AND PARSLEY

When serving mussels, simplicity is always the best option. The trick is to ensure that the shellfish retain the wonderful fresh flavour of the sea. In this recipe, the mussels are gently steamed in their shells with white wine, onion and garlic, and served moistened with the delicious cooking juices. Mussels are rich in the minerals iron, iodine and zinc and are a good source of the antioxidant trace mineral, selenium. They also contain small amounts of omega-3 fatty acids, known to be important for maintaining a healthy heart and circulation. Parsley is a rich source of the minerals iron and folate and the antioxidant vitamin beta-carotene. It also has a high natural chlorophyll content, making it an excellent breath freshener, particularly useful after eating garlic.

SERVES 4–6

1.5 kg/3 lb mussels in their shells, scrubbed and beards removed
4 tablespoons extra virgin olive oil
2 large onions, finely chopped
3 cloves garlic, finely chopped
450 ml/³⁄₄ pint dry white wine
juice of ¹⁄₂ lemon
freshly ground sea salt and black pepper
4 tablespoons finely chopped parsley
lemon wedges, to garnish

Discard any mussels that are not tightly closed. Warm the olive oil in a large saucepan and add the onion and garlic. Cover the saucepan and sweat the onion and garlic over a low heat for about 5 minutes, until soft and translucent, but not coloured. Pour the white wine into the pan and bring slowly to the boil. Add the mussels to the pan, cover and simmer over a moderate heat for about 5 minutes, until the mussel shells open. Discard any shells that do not open.

Drain the mussels and pile into warmed bowls. Bring the remaining cooking liquid to the boil, then add the lemon juice and boil over a moderate heat until reduced by about one-third, to concentrate the mussel flavours. Season to taste, then pour the cooking juices over the mussels. Sprinkle generously with chopped fresh parsley and garnish with lemon wedges.

SAUMON MARINE A L'ANETH

MARINATED SALMON WITH DILL

Fresh salmon in any form is a pleasure to eat, and this instant dish, requiring no cooking at all, owes its success to the exceptional quality of the fish. When I first tasted marinated salmon, I could not believe that something that takes only minutes to prepare could taste so amazing. Although the salmon is 'cooked' by the action of the lemon juice, it really is eaten raw, with the advantage that the nutritious content of the salmon remains intact: fresh salmon is an extremely valuable source of omega-3 essential fatty acids, nutrients that are wholly preserved in this dish.

SERVES 4

350 g/12 oz fillet of salmon, skinned
freshly squeezed juice of 2 lemons, strained
freshly ground sea salt and black pepper
4 tablespoons extra virgin olive oil
2–3 tablespoons finely chopped dill

Using a very sharp knife, carve the salmon into extremely fine slices, as if you were carving smoked salmon, then arrange the slices attractively on individual serving plates.

Sprinkle the lemon juice over the salmon, then season lightly with salt and plenty of black pepper. Drizzle the olive oil over the fish, then sprinkle generously with finely chopped dill. Leave to rest for 5–6 minutes to allow the marinade to work. During this time you will notice that the salmon changes colour and actually takes on the appearance of cooked salmon. Serve at once.

BRUSCHETTA AL POMODORO

TOASTED BREAD WITH TOMATOES, BASIL AND OLIVE OIL

These classic flavours appear over and over again in the Mediterranean diet. If you are looking for a nutritious and tasty snack, this bruschetta is the perfect answer. Bruschetta al Pomodoro is popular in trattorias throughout Italy, where garlic-scented toast is served oozing with tomatoes and basil drenched in olive oil.

SERVES 4

8 ripe tomatoes, skinned, seeded and diced
2 generous handfuls of basil leaves, torn into small pieces
freshly ground sea salt and black pepper
extra virgin olive oil
4 thick slices wholemeal country bread
2 cloves garlic, halved

Place the tomatoes in a bowl and add the basil leaves.

Season with salt and pepper, then pour on plenty of extra virgin olive oil.

Lightly toast the bread on both sides. Rub the cut sides of the garlic cloves over both sides of the bread, so that it is perfumed with the flavour of the garlic. Spoon the tomato and basil mixture over the toast and serve at once.

SALADE DE FROMAGE DE CHEVRE AUX POIVRONS

WARM SALAD OF GRILLED GOAT'S CHEESE WITH ROASTED SWEET PEPPERS

Fresh goat's cheese, an excellent source of calcium and protein, has a robust and aromatic flavour that is absolutely sensational just lightly warmed under a hot grill. It makes a beautiful starter served on a bed of salad leaves with roasted sweet peppers and a balsamic vinaigrette.

SERVES 4

2 large red peppers
1 large yellow pepper
1 large green pepper
350 g/12 oz goat's cheese, rind removed and cut into 4 slices
4 generous handfuls of mixed salad leaves, including rocket, radicchio and frisée

BALSAMIC DRESSING
175 ml/6 fl oz extra virgin olive oil
2 tablespoons balsamic vinegar
1/2 teaspoon Dijon mustard
1/2 teaspoon brown sugar
1 clove garlic, crushed
1 tablespoon finely chopped parsley
1 tablespoon finely chopped chervil
freshly ground sea salt and black pepper

Preheat the oven to 180°C/350°F/Gas Mark 4. Roast the peppers in the preheated oven for about 15 minutes, until the skins have blackened and blistered. Place the roasted peppers in a plastic bag and seal. When cool, peel off the skin, core and seed the peppers then cut into strips.

To make the dressing, whisk the olive oil and vinegar together until thoroughly emulsified. Add the Dijon mustard, sugar and garlic, mixing well. Mix in the fresh herbs, then season to taste with salt and pepper.

Place the goat's cheese slices under a hot grill for 2–3 minutes, until the cheese is glazed to a golden brown colour on top and just lightly warmed through.

To serve, arrange a nest of salad leaves in the centre of 4 individual serving plates, then lay the grilled goat's cheese on top. Arrange the roasted peppers around the cheese, then drizzle the vinaigrette all over the peppers. Serve at once with bruschetta, while still warm.

SALADE DE COQUILLES SAINT JACQUES A LA MANGUE

SALAD OF SCALLOPS WITH MANGO AND RASPBERRY-SCENTED DRESSING

Fresh scallops and exotic golden mango taste beautiful together. A hint of raspberry in the vinaigrette dressing brings out the flavour of the shellfish and the fruit in a most delicious way. Although not a native to the Mediterranean, the mango is a fruit that is enjoyed worldwide. It is also one of the richest fruit sources of antioxidant beta–carotene.

SERVES 4

150 ml/¹/₄ pint dry white wine
2 cloves garlic, finely chopped
freshly squeezed juice of ¹/₂ lemon
12 scallops with corals, shelled
4 generous handfuls of mixed salad leaves
2 ripe mangoes, peeled, stoned and chopped
125 g/4 oz raspberries, to garnish

RASPBERRY-SCENTED DRESSING
4 tablespoons extra virgin olive oil
2 tablespoons walnut oil
2 tablespoons raspberry vinegar
¹/₂ teaspoon Dijon mustard
¹/₂ teaspoon brown sugar
freshly ground sea salt and black pepper

Place the white wine, garlic and lemon juice in a large saucepan and bring slowly to the boil over a moderate heat. Reduce the heat to simmering point, then add the scallops and poach gently for about 1¹/₂ minutes, so that the scallops remain tender and moist. Remove the scallops with a slotted spoon and drain. Allow to cool, then cut each scallop into 3 slices, leaving the coral attached to one of the slices.

To prepare the dressing, whisk the olive oil, walnut oil and vinegar together until thoroughly emulsified, then add the Dijon mustard and sugar and mix well. Season to taste with salt and pepper.

Mix the salad leaves, mangoes and scallops together in a salad bowl, then pour over the dressing and toss well. Serve the salad on individual plates, garnished with fresh raspberries.

CALAMARES FRITOS A LA CATALANA

CATALAN-STYLE FRIED SQUID WITH GARLIC AND OLIVE OIL MAYONNAISE

Cataluna's very own mayonnaise, allioli, an intense mixture of garlic, olive oil and lemon juice, is served as an accompaniment to crisp, golden rings of deep-fried squid.

SERVES 4

500 g / 1 lb squid, cleaned and cut into 1 cm / ¹/₂ inch wide rings,
tentacles chopped
seasoned flour
vegetable oil, for deep-frying
lemon quarters, to garnish

ALLIOLI
6 cloves garlic
2 teaspoons freshly squeezed lemon juice
200 ml / 7 fl oz extra virgin olive oil
freshly ground sea salt and black pepper

To make the allioli, pound the garlic cloves to a smooth pulp using a pestle and mortar, then stir in the lemon juice. Slowly add the olive oil a drop at a time, blending well after each addition, until the mixture has a thick, creamy, mayonnaise-like consistency. Season to taste, then spoon into 4 small, individual pots.

Heat the oil in a deep pan to about 180°C/350°F, or until a cube of bread browns in 30 seconds. Dip the squid in the seasoned flour, then deep-fry in hot oil for about 1 minute, until golden brown. Remove with a slotted spoon and drain on kitchen paper. Serve hot, with lemon quarters, and a small pot of allioli for each person.

GAMBAS AL AJILLO

PRAWNS SAUTÉED IN OLIVE OIL WITH GARLIC AND CHILLI PEPPER

One of Spain's most popular dishes, this is often served in tapas bars and makes an absolutely terrific starter. The combination of shellfish, olive oil and garlic, so typical of Mediterranean cuisine, contains many of the important nutrients that are often linked to the region's low rate of heart disease and cancer.

SERVES 4

175 ml/6 fl oz extra virgin olive oil
4 cloves garlic, finely chopped
1 small red chilli pepper, seeded and finely chopped
freshly ground sea salt and black pepper
500 g/1 lb large raw prawns, shelled and deveined
3 tablespoons finely chopped parsley
lemon wedges, to garnish

Warm the olive oil in a large frying pan, then add the chopped garlic and chilli pepper. Season the oil with 2 twists of black pepper and 1 twist of sea salt, then sauté over a moderate heat for about 2 minutes, so that the oil is impregnated with the flavour of the garlic and chilli.

Add the prawns, stirring to ensure that they are well coated with the oil, then sauté for 2–3 minutes, until they turn a light pink colour, firm to the touch, but soft and succulent inside.

Transfer the prawns to warm serving dishes, then drizzle the hot, flavoured oil over them. Sprinkle with finely chopped parsley and garnish with lemon wedges.

COQUILLES SAINT JACQUES MER DU SUD

SCALLOPS WITH BLACK BEANS AND SWEET PEPPERS

I first tasted this succulent dish at a tiny, unadorned restaurant in Marseilles that served the most wonderful seafood. If you can, try to obtain scallops in their shells, so that the shells can be used as natural serving dishes.

SERVES 4

8 scallops in their shells, allowing 2 scallops per person
90 ml / 3 fl oz extra virgin olive oil
1 clove garlic, finely chopped
4 tablespoons dry white wine
150 ml / ¼ pint fish stock
1 tablespoon fermented black beans, finely chopped
1 tablespoon finely chopped red pepper, cored and seeded
1 tablespoon finely chopped green pepper, cored and seeded
freshly ground sea salt and black pepper

Using a knife with a rigid blade, prise open the scallop shells. Debeard the scallops, then rinse under cold water, leaving the corals intact, and pat dry. Thoroughly rinse and scrub 8 of the scallop shells for serving.

Warm the olive oil in a large frying pan, then add the scallops and garlic. Sear the scallops over a moderately high heat for just 1½ minutes, then remove from the pan with a slotted spoon and keep warm.

Pour the wine into the pan and stir to deglaze. Pour in the stock and boil until reduced by about one-third. When reduced, add the black beans and red and green peppers, then boil for a further 2 minutes, so that the vegetables are just tender. Adjust the seasoning. To serve, return the scallops to their shells, then spoon over the bean and pepper mixture.

PROSCUITTO CON FICHI NERO

RAW HAM WITH BLACK FIGS

One of Italy's most delicious exports, raw ham always makes a lovely, simple starter. Although traditionalists might question the modern trend of serving raw ham with fresh fruit, insisting that a really fine proscuitto should be eaten on its own, I feel that the lovely sweet flavour of fruit complements the slight saltiness of the proscuitto. When in season, black figs are wonderful served with proscuitto. Any type of melon, but especially canteloup, would also complement the flavour of the ham. A very popular fruit in the Mediterranean region, figs have for centuries been used as an ancient folk remedy.

SERVES 4

12 paper-thin slices of proscuitto
4 black figs

Arrange the proscuitto on individual serving plates. Cut each of the figs into 4 slices, then arrange decoratively, in a fan-like pattern, beside the ham. Serve at once.

HUEVOS A LA FLAMENCA

ANDALUSIAN-STYLE BAKED EGGS WITH VEGETABLES

When I lived in the enchanting city of Granada, evenings out often consisted of exciting visits to the gypsy caves hidden deep in the Sierra Nevada. Spectacular music and dancing accompanied the wine and wonderful food made from humble ingredients. In this gypsy recipe, eggs are baked in an earthenware dish nesting on a thick, well-flavoured vegetable stew know as *sofrito*, with some Serrano ham and chorizo thrown in to garnish. Even now, years later, when I prepare this dish at home, I can hear the gypsy music echoing in the background.

SERVES 4

4 tablespoons extra virgin olive oil
1 large onion, finely chopped
1 large potato, peeled and finely sliced
2 large red peppers, cored, seeded and cut into thin strips
4 cloves garlic, finely chopped
60 g/2 oz Serrano or other raw cured ham, finely chopped
8 tomatoes, skinned, seeded and coarsely chopped
125 g/4 oz shelled peas, preferably fresh
1 teaspoon paprika
freshly ground sea salt and black pepper
125 ml/4 fl oz water
4 eggs
8 slices chorizo sausage
8 fresh asparagus spears, steamed until just tender but still al dente
2 tablespoons finely chopped parsley

Warm the olive oil in a large frying pan, then add the chopped onion, potato, red peppers and garlic. Sauté over a low heat for about 5 minutes, until they begin to soften. Add half the chopped Serrano ham, then stir in the tomatoes, peas, and paprika, seasoning with salt and pepper. Stir in the water, then cover and simmer over a moderate heat for about 10 minutes.

Preheat the oven to 180°C/350°F/Gas Mark 4.

Pour the sofrito into a large, shallow earthenware dish, or into individual dishes, if preferred. Using the back of a spoon, make 4 hollows in the sofrito, then carefully break an egg into each hollow. Arrange the remaining ham, the chorizo and the asparagus spears over the dish, then sprinkle with finely chopped parsley.

Bake in the preheated oven for 8–10 minutes, until the whites of the egg are set, but the yolks still soft. Serve at once.

TORTILLA ESPANOLA

SPANISH OMELETTE WITH POTATOES, ONIONS AND GARLIC

Many of Spain's most popular and best-loved dishes have humble gypsy origins, which I think adds to the charm of this wonderful food. Prepared with simple ingredients, and once probably cooked outdoors over an open fire, with gypsy music echoing in the background, the tortilla española is a real gastronomic delight. Now almost a national dish, the tortilla is served in many different ways: hot, warm or cold, cut into wedges or in chunks, in tapas bars and at home, with and without garlic and parsley, and every Spanish lady will give you her own special recipe for making the perfect tortilla!

Although often underrated as fattening and non-nutritious, potatoes are in fact an exceptionally rich source of complex carbohydrates, the main suppliers of energy to the body, and provide valuable amounts of vitamin C, thiamin and potassium. They are also a good source of fibre.

SERVES 4–6

200 ml/7 fl oz extra virgin olive oil
500 g/1 lb potatoes, peeled and thinly sliced
2 large Spanish onions, finely chopped
2 cloves garlic, finely chopped
6 eggs
freshly ground sea salt and black pepper
2 tablespoons finely chopped parsley

Warm the olive oil in a large, non-stick frying pan, then add the potatoes, onions and garlic. Cover and sweat over a low heat for 25–30 minutes, until soft and translucent, but not coloured. Transfer the vegetables to a colander placed over a bowl, allowing the oil to drain off. Reserve the olive oil.

Lightly beat the eggs and season with salt and pepper. Stir the potato and onion mixture into the eggs.

Wipe the frying pan dry with kitchen paper, then pour in the reserved oil and warm gently. Pour in the tortilla mixture and cook over a low heat for about 8 minutes, without stirring, until the tortilla is almost set, brown on the underside but still slightly moist inside. Finish off by placing briefly under a medium-hot grill, to brown the top of the tortilla.

Slide the tortilla on to a large serving plate and sprinkle with finely chopped parsley. Serve either warm or cold, cut into wedges, accompanied by a crisp green salad.

TABBOULEH

HERB-SCENTED SALAD OF BURGHUL WHEAT AND TOMATOES

This combination of whole grains, tomatoes, onions and cucumber, flavoured with parsley, mint and lemon, gives a fresh-tasting salad. Whole grains are extremely nutritious and deserve to be given far greater prominence in our diet.

SERVES 4

125 g/4 oz burghul wheat
6 large ripe tomatoes, skinned, seeded and finely chopped
8 spring onions, finely chopped
7 cm/3 inch piece of cucumber, finely chopped
90 g/3 oz parsley, finely chopped
30 g/1 oz mint leaves, finely chopped
freshly squeezed juice of 1 lemon, strained
3 tablespoons extra virgin olive oil
freshly ground sea salt and black pepper
125 g/4 oz rocket leaves

Rinse the burghul wheat, then place in a large bowl and cover with cold water. Leave to soak and swell for about 25 minutes. Drain thoroughly, squeezing out excess moisture with your hands.

Stir the tomatoes, spring onions and cucumber into the burghul wheat, then add the parsley and mint. Mix together the lemon juice and olive oil and stir into the grains, seasoning to taste with salt and pepper.

Lay the rocket leaves on a serving platter, then pile the burghul salad on top.

POMODORI RIPIENI

STUFFED TOMATOES

Simple but impressive, stuffed tomatoes always make a lovely starter or light meal. A staple food in the Mediterranean diet, tomatoes are a rich source of three powerful antioxidant nutrients: vitamin C, beta-carotene and lycopene.

SERVES 4

8 large tomatoes
4 large mushrooms, finely chopped
2 shallots, finely chopped
2 tablespoons finely chopped parsley
2 tablespoons pine nuts
2 tablespoons wholemeal breadcrumbs
175 g/6 oz ricotta cheese
freshly ground sea salt and black pepper
watercress, to garnish

Preheat the oven to 180°C/350°F/Gas Mark 4.

Cut the tops off the tomatoes and reserve. Scoop out the seeds and flesh with a small teaspoon, leaving enough lining inside the tomatoes so that they do not disintegrate when baked. Dice the tomato flesh.

Mix together the mushrooms, shallots, parsley, pine nuts and breadcrumbs, then add to the diced tomato flesh. Fold the ricotta cheese into the mixture and season with salt and pepper.

Stuff the tomatoes with this mixture, then replace the reserved tops. Place in a lightly oiled ovenproof dish, cover with foil and bake in the preheated oven for about 15 minutes. Serve at once, garnished with watercress.

PAN BAGNAT

GARLIC-SCENTED ROLLS WITH PROVENÇAL SALAD

A speciality of Provence, *pan bagnat*, literally translated as 'moist bread', originates from the days when poor peasants working on the land used to mix pieces of stale bread into their salade Niçoise. The bread would be moistened by the olive oil and juices from the salad and made it into more of a hearty meal. Modern times have transformed pan bagnat into a delicious sandwich brimming with health–protecting nutrients, enjoyed not only by the farm workers, but by the rich and famous on the Mediterranean playground.

SERVES 4

4 large round crusty bread rolls, such as ciabatta
2 cloves garlic, halved
3 tablespoons extra virgin olive oil
4 tomatoes, cut into thin slices
1 red pepper, cored, seeded and cut lengthways into fine julienne strips
½ red onion, finely sliced
small piece of cucumber, finely sliced
250 g/8 oz tuna in olive oil, drained and flaked
generous handful of basil leaves, coarsely torn
125 g/4 oz pitted black olives
2 teaspoons red wine winegar
1 hard-boiled egg, cut into quarters
8 anchovy fillets in olive oil, drained
4 sprigs of basil

Slice the tops off the rolls and scoop out the soft centres. Rub the inside of the bread rolls with the cut side of the garlic cloves, so that the scent of the garlic is absorbed by the bread, then brush the bread shells lightly with some of the olive oil.

Mix together the tomatoes, red pepper, red onion and cucumber in a bowl. Add the flaked tuna, basil and half the black olives. Pile the salad mixture into the bread shells.

Mix the remaining olive oil with the wine vinegar, then drizzle lightly over the salad. Arrange the hard-boiled egg, anchovies and remaining black olives on top, then replace the tops of the rolls. Leave to rest for about 1 hour before serving, so that the flavours can mingle and moisten the bread. Garnish with sprigs of basil just before serving.

CALAMARI RIPIENI

STUFFED SQUID

Squid is a popular appetizer in the Mediterranean, in particular in Italy and Spain. A good balance of protein, vitamins, minerals and complex carbohydrates is contained in this tasty Italian dish.

SERVES 6

6 large squid, cleaned and tentacles reserved
1 kg/2 lb tomatoes, skinned, seeded and finely chopped
90 ml/3 fl oz dry white wine
2–3 tablespoons extra virgin olive oil
sprigs of basil, to garnish

STUFFING
1 tablespoon extra virgin olive oil
1 medium onion, finely chopped
1 clove garlic, finely chopped
1 red pepper, cored, seeded and finely diced
125 g/4 oz long-grain rice
90 g/3 oz pine nuts
2 tablespoons finely chopped parsley
freshly ground sea salt and black pepper
175 ml/6 fl oz water

To make the stuffing, heat the olive oil in a saucepan, add the onion, garlic and red pepper, and sweat over a low heat until soft and translucent, but not coloured. Stir in the rice, pine nuts and chopped parsley, seasoning with salt and pepper. Pour in the water, then cover and cook over a moderate heat, without stirring, for about 10 minutes, until all the liquid has been absorbed.

Preheat the oven to 180°C/350°F/Gas Mark 4.

Stuff each squid about three-quarters full with the rice mixture, allowing room for it to swell up while cooking. Close up the open ends of the squid with wooden cocktail sticks.

Spread out the chopped tomatoes in a large ovenproof baking dish, and season with salt and pepper. Pour over the dry white wine. Arrange the stuffed squid and the reserved tentacles over the tomatoes, then drizzle with olive oil. Cover with baking foil, then bake in the preheated oven for about 15 minutes.

Arrange the stuffed squid on individual warm serving plates. Place the tomatoes in a blender or food processor and purée until smooth. Adjust the seasoning. Spoon the puréed tomatoes around the squid, and garnish with the tentacles and sprigs of fresh basil.

ASPERGES A LA VINAIGRETTE

ASPARAGUS VINAIGRETTE

Fresh, lightly steamed asparagus, rich in vitamin E, needs nothing more than a simple lemon and walnut flavoured vinaigrette to complement it perfectly.

SERVES 4

24 asparagus spears, trimmed
1–2 tablespoons finely chopped flat-leaf parsley

LEMON AND WALNUT VINAIGRETTE
4 tablespoons extra virgin olive oil
2 tablespoons walnut oil
2 tablespoons freshly squeezed lemon juice
½ teaspoon Dijon mustard
freshly ground sea salt and black pepper

Tie the asparagus into bundles, securing with string, then stand upright in a saucepan containing about 5 cm/2 inches of lightly salted water. Bring to the boil, then cover and steam for about 10 minutes, until tender but not too soft or disintegrating.

Meanwhile, prepare the vinaigrette. Whisk the olive oil, walnut oil and lemon juice together until thoroughly emulsified. Mix in the Dijon mustard and season to taste with salt and pepper.

Serve the asparagus lukewarm, dressed with the lemon and walnut vinaigrette and sprinkled very lightly with finely chopped parsley.

PIPERADE

SCRAMBLED EGGS WITH SWEET PEPPERS, ONIONS AND TOMATOES

With its simple yet clever usage of eggs and vegetables, this Provençal speciality has achieved world-wide popularity. Cooked in this way, the eggs absorb the lovely sweet flavour and aroma of the peppers and tomatoes, and make a delicious light lunch dish.

SERVES 4

4 tablespoons extra virgin olive oil
2 large onions, finely chopped
3 large red peppers, cored, seeded and cut lengthways into fine strips
2 cloves garlic, finely chopped
250 g/8 oz ripe tomatoes, skinned, seeded and finely chopped
freshly ground sea salt and black pepper
6 eggs, lightly beaten

Warm the olive oil in a large frying pan, then add the onions. Cover and sweat over a low heat for about 5 minutes, until soft and translucent.

Add the red peppers and garlic and continue to sauté over a gentle heat for a further 5 minutes, until the peppers are soft. Add the tomatoes and cook gently for 3–4 minutes. Season with salt and pepper.

Remove from the heat and allow to cool slightly, then pour the beaten eggs on to the sautéed vegetables. Return to a low heat and cook gently for 2-3 minutes, stirring constantly, until the eggs have scrambled. Serve accompanied by some salad leaves.

SALADE DE CALMARES AUX ANCHOIS

WARM SALAD OF GRILLED SQUID WITH ANCHOVY DRESSING

Squid makes a lovely meal just lightly grilled, and even better char-grilled. Here the squid is served in a mouth-watering warm salad with spinach leaves, crisp broccoli florets and carrot julienne, dressed with a superb vinaigrette flavoured with anchovies, garlic and parsley.
A high intake of antioxidant nutrients such as those provided by the vegetables in this salad is believed to protect the body against the damaging effects of excess free radicals.

SERVES 4

4 squid, cleaned, opened out flat and cut into 6 squares
1 tablespoon extra virgin olive oil
freshly ground sea salt and black pepper
125 g/4 oz broccoli florets
4 small carrots, cut into julienne strips
175 g/6 oz spinach leaves, tough stalks removed

ANCHOVY DRESSING
175 g/6 oz anchovy fillets in olive oil, drained
6 tablespoons milk
1 clove garlic, finely chopped
3 tablespoons finely chopped parsley
1 tablespoon freshly squeezed lemon juice
175 ml/6 fl oz extra virgin olive oil
freshly ground black pepper

Begin by preparing the anchovy dressing. Soak the fillets in milk for 10 minutes, to extract excessive saltiness, then remove and pat dry on kitchen paper. Pound the anchovies, garlic and 2 tablespoons of parsley together to a smooth paste, using a pestle and mortar, then gradually incorporate the lemon juice. Add the olive oil in a thin stream, mixing well until thoroughly emulsified, then season with black pepper.

Brush the squid lightly with olive oil and season on both sides with salt and pepper.

Steam the broccoli and carrot together over boiling water for about 2 minutes, until tender but still al dente.

Grill the squid pieces under a hot grill for about 2 minutes, turning once.

To serve, arrange the spinach leaves on individual serving plates, then place the grilled squid and steamed vegetables on top. Drizzle the anchovy dressing over the salad, then sprinkle with the remaining parsley.

TAPENADE

BLACK OLIVE, CAPER AND ANCHOVY PASTE

Tapenade is an exotic-flavoured Provençal paste made from a delicious blend of black olives, capers and anchovies. It derives its name from the word *tapena*, which in local Provençal dialect means capers. It makes a mouthwatering appetizer served simply on thin slices of toasted wholemeal bread and is popularly used as an unusually flavoursome filling for hard-boiled eggs.

350 g/12 oz black olives, pitted
125 g/4 oz capers, rinsed
8 anchovy fillets in olive oil, drained
1 clove garlic, crushed
1 tablespoon coarsely torn basil leaves
2 teaspoons freshly squeezed lemon juice
4–5 tablespoons extra virgin olive oil
freshly ground black pepper

Place all the ingredients except the olive oil and black pepper in a food processor or blender and process until smooth. With the motor still running, slowly pour in the olive oil, adding sufficient to give a smooth, thick, paste-like consistency. Season generously with black pepper.

ANCHOÏADE

ANCHOVY AND GARLIC PASTE

Another wonderful Provençal delicacy, which, as the name suggests, is an intensely flavoured blend of anchovies and garlic. Spread simply on thin triangles of warm toast, anchoïade makes a lovely accompaniment to a glass of wine. For a light lunch, drizzle some olive oil on a slice of wholemeal country bread, spread generously with anchoïade, then place under a hot grill for 1 minute and serve hot. It also makes a good glaze for grilled chicken or roast lamb, bringing a delightful Mediterranean flavour to simple food.

20 anchovy fillets in olive oil, drained
milk, for soaking
2 cloves garlic, crushed
6–8 tablespoons extra virgin olive oil
1 tablespoon freshly squeezed lemon juice
freshly ground black pepper

Soak the anchovy fillets in milk for about 10 minutes. This will remove excessive saltiness, without taking away the flavour of the anchovies. Drain the anchovies and squeeze dry with your hands. Place in a food processor or blender with the garlic cloves, and process until smooth. With the motor still running, slowly add sufficient oil to give a smooth, thick, paste-like consistency. Add the lemon juice and season generously with black pepper. Anchoïade will keep in the refrigerator for up to 10 days in a sealed container.

TARAMASALATA

SMOKED COD'S ROE APPETIZER

This savoury appetizer, of Greek or Turkish origin, is served as a dip with crunchy raw vegetables, or as a starter, served with black olives and toasted wholemeal country bread. Originally, the appetizer was made with *tarama*, the salted and dried roe of the grey mullet, but over the years, smoked cod's roe has become a more popular ingredient. There are many variations on how to make taramasalata – some use mashed potato, cream cheese or yoghurt instead of bread, but this recipe is, I feel, closest to the original, classic taramasalata.

125 g / 4 oz smoked cod's roe
freshly squeezed juice of 1 large lemon
2 cloves garlic, crushed
2 thick slices of Olive Oil Bread (see page 244), crusts removed
6–8 tablespoons extra virgin olive oil
freshly ground sea salt and black pepper

Remove the skin from the roe, then place in a food processor or blender with the lemon juice and garlic. Soak the bread in cold water, to moisten, then squeeze dry with your hands. Add the bread to the roe and other ingredients, then process to give a smooth paste.

With the motor still running, slowly pour in the olive oil, adding sufficient to give a thick, mayonnaise-like consistency. Season to taste.

4

Fish and Shellfish

SARDINAS ANDALUZAS

ANDALUSIAN-STYLE FRESH SARDINES WITH LEMON JUICE, WINE, GARLIC AND PARSLEY

Fresh sardines have a sweet flesh and are really delicious quickly pan-fried in olive oil with garlic, then moistened with lemon juice and white wine. This simple yet special way of cooking sardines is a speciality of Granada. Research has shown that eating as little as three portions a week of an oily fish such as sardines can help to maintain a healthy heart.

SERVES 4

1 kg/2 lb sardines, scaled, with heads left on
2 tablespoons flour
6 tablespoons extra virgin olive oil
2 cloves garlic, finely chopped
150 ml/¹/₄ pint dry white wine
freshly squeezed juice of 2 large lemons
4 tablespoons finely chopped parsley
freshly ground sea salt and black pepper

Season the sardines all over with salt and pepper, then dust very lightly with flour.

Warm the olive oil in a large frying pan, then add the garlic. Sweat over a moderate heat for about 2 minutes, to soften the garlic and flavour the oil. Lay the sardines in the oil and sauté over a moderate heat for 2–3 minutes, turning once. Pour the white wine and lemon juice over the sardines and simmer over a low heat for 4–5 minutes. Sprinkle generously with chopped parsley and serve either warm or cold.

COQUILLES SAINT JACQUES A LA PROVENCALE

SEARED SCALLOPS WITH PROVENÇAL SAUCE

Basil, tomatoes, olive oil and garlic give a classic Provençal flavour to these succulent seared scallops. Low in saturated fat, scallops are a good source of protein, vitamin B12 and the important antioxidant trace mineral, selenium.

SERVES 4

6 tablespoons extra virgin olive oil
16 scallops, shelled
500 g / 1 lb tomatoes, skinned, seeded and finely chopped
2 cloves garlic, finely chopped
generous handful of basil leaves, coarsely torn
2 tablespoons dry white wine
freshly ground sea salt and black pepper
lemon wedges, to garnish
sprigs of fresh basil, to garnish

Warm 2 tablespoons of olive oil in a large frying pan. Pat the scallops dry on kitchen paper, then season lightly. Place in the frying pan and sear over a high heat for slightly less than 1 minute on each side, so that the scallops are just lightly cooked and remain succulent and moist. Remove from the pan and keep warm.

Add the remaining olive oil to the frying pan, then add the tomatoes and garlic. Sauté over a moderate heat for about 2 minutes, then add the basil leaves and white wine. Season with salt and pepper, and cook for 1 more minute.

Spoon the tomato and basil mixture on to warm serving plates, then lay the seared scallops on top. Garnish with lemon wedges and sprigs of basil.

FILETS DE SAUMON A L'ANETH

FILLETS OF SALMON WITH DILL VINAIGRETTE

Salmon and dill make a perfect partnership. The salmon is flavoured with lemon-scented olive oil before grilling, then served on a bed of spinach, with a dill vinaigrette.

SERVES 4

4 fillets of salmon
500 g / 1 lb baby spinach leaves, tough stalks removed

LEMON-SCENTED OIL
4 tablespoons extra virgin olive oil
3 strips finely pared lemon zest

DILL VINAIGRETTE
6 tablespoons extra virgin olive oil
2 tablespoons white wine vinegar
$1/2$ teaspoon Dijon mustard
$1/2$ teaspoon brown sugar
2 tablespoons finely chopped dill
freshly ground sea salt and black pepper

To prepare the lemon-scented oil, place the oil and lemon zest in a screw-topped jar, then shake well and leave for 2 hours, so that the flavour is absorbed by the oil.

To make the vinaigrette, whisk the olive oil and vinegar until thoroughly emulsified. Add the mustard and sugar, mixing well, then add the chopped dill and season to taste.

Brush the salmon with the oil, then grill under a moderate heat for about 2 minutes on each side, making sure it is not over-cooked, and remains moist inside.

Rinse the spinach leaves, then place in a large saucepan, seasoning lightly. Cover and leave to wilt over a moderate heat for 2–3 minutes. Spoon the spinach on to individual plates, then lay the salmon on top. Drizzle with the dill vinaigrette.

LOUP DE MER AU FOUR

BAKED SEA BASS WITH FENNEL

The anise flavour of fennel is a perfect partner for this baked sea bass, served here with a crisp, lightly charred skin. A dash of Pernod enhances this wonderful blend of flavours.

SERVES 4

4 sea bass, about 350 g / 12 oz each, scaled
freshly ground sea salt and black pepper
6 tablespoons extra virgin olive oil
4 fennel bulbs, sliced, with feathery leaves reserved
4 cloves garlic, crushed
4 red onions, sliced into rings
freshly squeezed juice of 1 lemon
90 ml / 3 fl oz Pernod
lemon wedges and sprigs of flat-leaf parsley, to garnish

Season the sea bass inside and out with salt and pepper. Brush the skin lightly with olive oil. Chop the reserved fennel leaves, mix with the garlic and place inside the fish cavities. Place the sea bass under a hot grill and grill for about 3–4 minutes on each side, so that the skin is crisp and lightly charred.

Preheat the oven to 190°C/375°F/Gas Mark 5.

Place the fennel and red onions in a large, lightly oiled ovenproof roasting dish, then lay the sea bass on top. Pour over the lemon juice, olive oil and Pernod and bake for about 15 minutes, until the flesh is firm to the touch.

Spoon the onions and fennel on to individual serving plates, then lay the sea bass on top. Drizzle some of the cooking juices over the fish and garnish with lemon wedges and sprigs of parsley.

SOGLIOLA ALLA TOSCANA

SOLE TUSCAN STYLE

This classic style of light cooking suits sole perfectly. In this recipe, the fish is quickly sautéed, then laced with lemon juice and fresh parsley, and finally moistened with the garlic-scented olive oil cooking juices.

Unlike oily fish, whose flesh is a rich source of fatty acids, white fish such as sole store these essential oils in the liver, so always buy sole unfilleted, with the liver intact.

SERVES 2

2 soles, trimmed, with head and tail removed but left unfilleted,
with the liver intact
90 ml / 3 fl oz milk
2 tablespoons plain flour, seasoned with freshly ground sea salt
and black pepper
150 ml / ¼ pint olive oil
1 clove garlic
freshly squeezed juice of 2 large lemons
3 tablespoons finely chopped parsley
lemon wedges, to garnish

Dip the sole in milk, then in the seasoned flour, shaking off any excess.

Place 6 tablespoons of olive oil in a large frying pan with the garlic clove. Warm over a moderate heat, swirling the garlic around in the oil to flavour it. Sauté the sole in the oil for about 6 minutes, turning once, until golden on both sides. If the sole are quite large, you will need to cook each fish separately.

Transfer the sole to individual serving plates. Drizzle the lemon juice over each sole, then sprinkle generously with chopped parsley. Keep warm.

Gazpacho (Spain)
A chilled vegetable soup served with
garnish and croûtons
p7

Insalata di Peperoni alla Napoletana (Italy)
A roasted red and yellow pepper salad
with anchovies, capers and garlic
p45

Salade de Fromage de Chèvre aux Poivrons (France)
A warm salad of grilled goat's cheese
with roasted sweet peppers
p76

Gambas a la Plancha (Spain)
Grilled Mediterranean prawns with baby artichokes
p116

Triglia alla Griglia (Italy)
Grilled red mullet with red peppers and green sauce
p124

Sardine in Foglie Di Vite (Italy)
Sardines wrapped in vine leaves and grilled
p135

Pollo al Ajillo (Spain)
Sherry-scented chicken with thirty cloves of garlic
p146

Rigatoni con i Broccoli (Italy)
Rigatoni pasta with broccoli, anchovies and black olives
p164

Add the remaining oil to the frying pan and warm over a moderate heat. Moisten the fish with the warm, garlic-scented olive oil and serve at once, garnished with lemon wedges.

CABALLA EN ESCABECHE

ESCABECHE OF MARINATED MACKEREL

This classic Spanish method of marinating mackerel in olive oil and sherry vinegar, with fresh herbs and vegetables, makes an inexpensive fish taste very special.
Mackerel's oily flesh contains exceptionally high levels of essential omega-3 fatty acids, protective oils that are highly beneficial to the heart and circulatory system.

SERVES 4

8 mackerel fillets
freshly ground sea salt and black pepper
2 tablespoons plain flour
200 ml/7 fl oz extra virgin olive oil
1 large onion, finely chopped
3 cloves garlic, finely chopped
2 large carrots, finely chopped
2 tablespoons finely chopped parsley
1 bay leaf
1 teaspoon chopped thyme
125 ml/4 fl oz sherry vinegar
90 ml/3 fl oz water

Pat the mackerel fillets dry, then season all over with salt and pepper. Dust the fillets lightly with flour.

Warm half the olive oil in a large frying pan, then sauté the fish over a moderately high heat for about 1½ minutes on each side, until golden brown. Remove with a slotted spoon and place in a shallow dish.

Add the remaining olive oil to the pan, then add the onion, garlic and carrots and sauté over a moderate heat until soft but not coloured. Add the parsley, bay leaf and thyme. Pour in the sherry vinegar, allowing it to bubble and absorb the cooking juices, then add the water and simmer for several minutes to allow all the flavours to infuse together. Season to taste.

Pour the herb and sherry-scented liquid and vegetables over the mackerel, then cover and leave the fish to marinate for several hours. Serve with a crisp green salad.

COQUILLES SAINT JACQUES A LA NICOISE

GRILLED SCALLOPS WITH MEDITERRANEAN VEGETABLE RAGÔUT

This exquisite dish is rich in the wonderful flavours that are typical of the South of France. The scallops are quickly grilled, then served over a fine ragôut of Mediterranean vegetables, and dressed with a Niçoise-style dressing, complementing the delicate flavour of the scallops.

SERVES 4

10 scallops, shelled, without corals
freshly ground sea salt and black pepper
4 generous handfuls of mixed salad leaves such as frisée, radicchio,
lamb's lettuce and rocket

VEGETABLE RAGOUT
3 tablespoons extra virgin olive oil
1 red pepper, cored, seeded and diced
1/2 green pepper, cored, seeded and diced
1/2 yellow pepper, cored, seeded and diced
60 g/2 oz courgettes, diced
60 g/2 oz aubergines, diced
1 clove garlic, finely chopped
2 tomatoes, skinned, seeded and diced

BASIL-SCENTED DRESSING
125 ml/4 fl oz extra virgin olive oil
2 teaspoons white wine vinegar
2 generous handfuls of basil leaves

Cut each scallop into 2 pieces, pat dry, then season with salt and pepper.

To make the dressing, gently warm the olive oil and vinegar together over a low heat, then remove from the heat and add the basil leaves. Season with salt and pepper, then place in a food processor or blender and process until smooth. Set the dressing aside to cool.

To prepare the vegetable ragout, heat the oil in a saucepan and add the peppers, courgettes, aubergines and garlic. Sauté for 3–4 minutes until just tender, adding the diced tomatoes during the last minute.

Place the scallops under a hot grill and grill for just 20 seconds on each side, so that they remain succulent and moist.

To serve, arrange the salad leaves in the centre of individual serving plates. Place 5 small spoonfuls of the vegetable ragôut in a circle around the salad leaves on each plate, topping each spoonful of vegetables with a piece of grilled scallop. Drizzle the basil dressing around the scallops and serve at once.

ROUGET A LA PROVENCALE

PROVENÇAL-STYLE RED MULLET WITH MEDITERRANEAN VEGETABLES

Red mullet has a lovely sweet flesh and beautiful pink colour. In traditional Provençal style, the fish is best grilled whole on the bone, gutted but the liver left intact, as this is considered a great delicacy. Red mullet is an excellent source of protein and vitamins A, B12 and D, as well as the minerals iron and zinc.

SERVES 4

4 red mullet, scaled, with liver left intact
freshly ground sea salt and black pepper
2 aubergines, sliced crossways
2 large courgettes, sliced
1 large red pepper, cored, seed and sliced lenthways into 2.5 cm/
1 inch slices
1 large yellow pepper, cored, seeded and cut lengthways into
2.5 cm/1 inch slices
1 clove garlic, crushed
3 tablespoons extra virgin olive oil

LEMON AND HERB DRESSING
6 tablespoons extra virgin olive oil
freshly squeezed juice of 1 lemon
$\frac{1}{2}$ teaspoon Dijon mustard
1 tablespoon finely chopped chervil
1 tablespoon finely chopped flat-leaf parsley
freshly ground sea salt and black pepper

Rinse the mullet well then pat dry and season inside and out with salt and pepper.

Place the sliced aubergines in a nylon colander and sprinkle with salt. Leave to rest for about 30 minutes, to draw out the bitter juices. Preheat the oven to 180°C/350°F/Gas Mark 4.

Place all the vegetables in a large roasting dish. Mix the garlic with the oil and drizzle over the vegetables. Roast in the preheated oven for about 15 minutes.

To make the dressing, whisk the olive oil and lemon juice together until thoroughly emulsified, then add the Dijon mustard and herbs, mixing well. Season to taste.

Lay the red mullet on a lightly oiled grill pan, then grill under a moderately high heat for 4–5 minutes on each side.

To serve, arrange the roasted vegetables in a circle, on individual serving plates. Lay the grilled red mullet over the vegetables, then drizzle the dressing around the vegetables.

CALAMARES A LA PLANCHA CON LIMON Y PEREJIL

GRILLED SQUID WITH LEMON AND PARSLEY

Squid is an extremely popular dish in Spain and is served in countless ways in tapas bars, restaurants and at home. A good source of protein with a low saturated fat content, squid makes an ideal choice for a light, nutritious dish. In this simple recipe, the sharp, robust flavours of lemon and parsley marry beautifully with the subtle taste of the grilled squid.

SERVES 4

4 squid, cleaned, opened out flat and cut into 6 even-sized pieces, tentacles reserved
2 tablespoons extra virgin olive oil
freshly ground sea salt and black pepper
4 generous handfuls of mixed salad leaves, including rocket
lemon halves, to garnish

LEMON AND PARSLEY DRESSING
175 ml/6 fl oz extra virgin olive oil
1 clove garlic, crushed
freshly squeezed juice of 1 large lemon, strained
½ teaspoon Dijon mustard
2 tablespoons finely chopped parsley

To make the dressing, place the olive oil in a small saucepan and add the tentacles and garlic. Warm the olive oil very gently over a low heat, then leave to infuse for about 10 minutes, so that the flavours are absorbed by the oil.

Remove the tentacles with a slotted spoon and reserve, then stir in the lemon juice and Dijon mustard, mixing well until thoroughly emulsified. Add the chopped parsley, then season to taste with salt and pepper.

Brush the squid pieces lightly with olive oil, then season with salt and pepper. Grill the squid pieces and tentacles under a hot grill for 2–3 minutes, turning once.

To serve, arrange a bed of salad leaves on individual serving plates, then lay the grilled squid on top. Drizzle the lemon and parsley dressing over and around the squid and salad leaves. Garnish with lemon halves, tied up in muslin.

GAMBAS A LA PLANCHA

GRILLED GARLIC-SCENTED MEDITERRANEAN PRAWNS

These succulent grilled prawns are laced with garlic-scented oil and combined with the wonderful earthy flavour of grilled artichokes to make a superb meal. Serve with salad, saffron rice or couscous. If you are unable to find baby artichokes, large ones will do, but cut the artichokes into eighths rather than quarters. Prawns are an excellent source of protein and vitamin B12.

SERVES 4

24 large raw prawns, shelled and deveined, with tails left on
2 cloves garlic, crushed
4 tablespoons extra virgin olive oil
4 baby artichokes, boiled until tender, but still firm
freshly ground sea salt and black pepper

Place the prawns in a shallow dish and season lightly. Mix the garlic into the olive oil and pour over the prawns, making sure that they are all thoroughly coated. Cover and leave to marinate for about 30 minutes.

Cut each of the baby artichokes into quarters. Drain the prawns, reserving the marinade. Thread 3 prawns and 2 pieces of artichoke on to each skewer, ready for grilling. Brush the artichokes lightly with some of the reserved marinade.

Place the skewers under a very hot grill and grill for 1½–2 minutes on each side, turning once. Serve the prawns on a bed of couscous, with salad.

FILETS DE MAQUEREAU AU CERFEUIL

FILLETS OF MACKEREL WITH CHERVIL

The strong flavours of chervil and lemon are in perfect harmony with the oily flesh of fresh mackerel, one of the richest sources of omega-3 fatty acids.

SERVES 4

4 mackerel fillets, about 125 g/4 oz each
2 tablespoons seasoned flour
125 ml/4 fl oz extra virgin olive oil
freshly squeezed juice of 1 lemon
1 tablespoon dry white vermouth
2 tablespoons chopped chervil leaves
12 asparagus spears, steamed over boiling water until tender but
still al dente

Dust the mackerel fillets lightly with the seasoned flour, shaking off any excess. Warm half the olive oil in a large frying pan, then sauté the mackerel quickly in the oil for about 2 minutes on each side, until golden brown. Remove the mackerel from the pan with a slotted spoon and keep warm.

Pour off all the oil remaining in the frying pan, then add the lemon juice, vermouth and remaining olive oil to the pan. Warm gently together then remove from the heat and add the fresh chervil.

To serve, arrange the mackerel fillets on warm serving plates with the asparagus spears, then drizzle the lemon and chervil dressing over the fish.

KEBAB SAMAK

MARINATED FISH KEBABS

A perfect al fresco dish for balmy summer evenings, even
better cooked on a barbecue if possible. Firm-fleshed fish
such as salmon, tuna and monkfish are ideal for kebabs.
Grilling is a healthy cooking medium for fish, ensuring
that all the valuable oils and nutrients are preserved.

SERVES 4

*350 g / 12 oz salmon fillets, skinned and boned and cut into
4 cm / 1½ inch cubes*
*350 g / 12 oz fresh tuna, boned and cut into 4 cm / 1½ inch
cubes*
12 raw prawns, shelled and deveined
8 bay leaves
lemon wedges, to serve

MARINADE
4 tablespoons extra virgin olive oil
freshly squeezed juice of 1 large lemon
1 clove garlic, finely chopped
1 tablespoon finely chopped chives
1 tablespoon finely chopped parsley
freshly ground sea salt and black pepper

Place the fish in a bowl with the prawns. To make the
marinade, whisk the olive oil and lemon juice together until
thoroughly emulsified, then add the garlic, chives and parsley.
Season, then pour over the fish. Leave to marinate for about 2
hours, stirring from time to time.

Drain the fish and thread on to skewers, alternating with
the prawns and bay leaves. Place under a hot grill for 3–4
minutes on each side. Serve with lemon wedges.

LOUP DE MER AUX OIGNONS ROUGES

ROAST SEA BASS WITH RED ONIONS IN RED WINE

Sea bass has a delicate flavour and texture and the slightly sweet taste of the wine-infused red onions complements the fish beautifully.

SERVES 4

4 sea bass fillets, about 175 g/6 oz each, skin left on, but scaled
4 tablespoons extra virgin olive oil

RED ONIONS IN RED WINE
350 g/12 oz red onions, finely sliced
175 ml/6 fl oz dry red wine
freshly ground sea salt and black pepper
pared strip of orange zest, cut into tiny julienne strips and blanched in boiling water
1 teaspoon clear honey
4 sprigs of chervil, to garnish

Place the onions in a large heavy-based saucepan, then pour over the red wine, seasoning lightly. Place over a moderate heat and simmer gently until the onions are soft and all the wine has been absorbed. Stir in the orange zest and honey. Preheat the oven to 200°C/400°F/Gas Mark 6.

Season the sea bass lightly. Warm the olive oil in a large frying pan, then sear the sea bass briefly over a high heat for about 1 minute on each side. Transfer the fish, skin-side up, to a lightly oiled ovenproof dish and roast for 6 minutes, so that it is crisp on the outside, but moist inside.

To serve, spoon the red onions on to warm serving plates, then lay the sea bass on top. Garnish with sprigs of chervil.

ZARZUELA

SEAFOOD CASSEROLE

Seafood casseroles are a speciality of the Mediterranean, where different varieties of fish and shellfish are tossed into a casserole dish with vegetables, stock, wine and herbs. Whilst extremely simple to make, the finished dish is sensational, rich in all the wonderful flavours of the sea. Low in saturated fat, fish and shellfish in this dish are valuable sources of protein, and provide a range of important vitamins and minerals, including vitamin D, B12, iodine, selenium and zinc.

SERVES 4

4 tablespoons extra virgin olive oil
2 large onions, finely chopped
6 cloves garlic, finely chopped
1 kg/2 lb tomatoes, skinned, seeded and coarsely chopped
1 teaspoon fennel seeds
150 ml/¼ pint dry white wine
350 ml/12 fl oz fish stock
½ teaspoon saffron strands
1 bay leaf
1 sprig of fresh thyme
250 g/8 oz squid, cleaned and sliced into rings, tentacles chopped
250 g/8 oz large raw prawns in their shells
8 mussels, scrubbed and beards removed
8 clams, scrubbed
4 small red mullet, scaled
freshly ground sea salt and black pepper
4 tablespoons finely chopped parsley

Warm the olive oil in a large casserole dish, then add the onions and garlic. Sweat over a low heat for about 5 minutes, until soft and translucent, but not coloured. Add the tomatoes and fennel seeds, and cook over a gentle heat for about 10 minutes, until the tomatoes are reduced to a thick pulp.

Pour in the white wine, fish stock, saffron, bay leaf and thyme, and bring slowly to the boil. Reduce the heat to simmering point, then add all the shellfish and fish. Cover the casserole then simmer gently for about 15 minutes. Adjust the seasoning and add the fresh parsley. Serve straight from the casserole, accompanied by some wholemeal country bread.

FILETS DE SAUMON MISTRAL

FILLETS OF SALMON WITH BABY SPINACH, TOMATOES AND BASIL OIL

The south of France has created some sensational fish dishes - too many to include in this book. But this particular recipe, using that familiar Mediterranean combination of wilted spinach, tomatoes, garlic and basil, is just too wonderful to leave out.

SERVES 4

3 tablespoons extra virgin olive oil
2 shallots, finely diced
350 g / 12 oz tomatoes, skinned, seeded and diced
500 g / 1 lb baby spinach, tough stalks removed
freshly ground sea salt and black pepper
4 salmon fillets, skinned and boned

BASIL OIL
freshly squeezed juice of 1 lemon
175 ml / 6 fl oz extra virgin olive oil
1 clove garlic, crushed
2 generous handfuls of basil leaves, cut into fine strips

Heat 1 tablespoon of olive oil in a frying pan and sauté the shallots over a low heat until soft and translucent, but not coloured. Add the diced tomatoes to the shallots and sauté for 1 more minute.

Rinse the spinach, then place in a large saucepan, season with salt and pepper, cover and leave to wilt over a moderate heat for about 3 minutes.

Warm 2 tablespoons of olive oil in a large frying pan, then sauté the salmon fillets over a moderate heat for about 2-3 minutes on each side, depending on their thickness, making sure that the fillets remain moist inside.

Remove from the pan with a slotted spoon and keep warm.

To make the basil oil, pour off any oil remaining in the frying pan, then add the lemon juice and the olive oil. Warm gently so that the oil is infused with the aroma of the fish cooking juices, then add the garlic and basil leaves and a twist of salt and black pepper. Warm gently for 1 more minute to allow the flavours to mingle.

To serve, place a nest of wilted spinach in the centre of individual warm serving plates, then spoon the tomato and shallot mixture on top. Lay the salmon fillets over the tomatoes and spinach, then spoon the basil oil over the fish and vegetables. Serve at once.

TRIGLIA ALLA GRIGLIA

GRILLED RED MULLET WITH RED PEPPERS AND GREEN SAUCE

Richly flavoured with fresh herbs, garlic and olive oil, this wonderfully fragrant green sauce make a delicious accompaniment to all varieties of grilled fish, but marries particularly well with the sweet pink flesh of the red mullet.

SERVES 4

4 red mullet, scaled, with liver left intact
freshly ground sea salt and black pepper
2 tablespoons extra virgin olive oil
4 red peppers, cored, seeded and halved

GREEN SAUCE
3 tablespoons roughly chopped parsley
2 tablespoons coarsely torn basil leaves
3 cloves garlic, coarsely chopped
2 tablespoons chopped capers, rinsed and drained
6 anchovy fillets in olive oil, soaked in milk for 10 minutes, then squeezed dry and coarsely chopped
1 teaspoon Dijon mustard
freshly squeezed juice of 1 lemon
175 ml/6 fl oz extra virgin olive oil
freshly ground sea salt and black pepper

To make the green sauce, place all the ingredients except the olive oil in a blender or food processor and blend well until smooth. With the machine still running, slowly add the olive oil in a thin stream, blending well to obtain a thick, green homogenous consistency. Season generously with black pepper.

Season the mullet with salt and pepper. Brush lightly all over with olive oil, then lay the fish on a large grill pan. Lay the red peppers, skin-side up, alongside the fish. Place under a hot grill and grill the fish for about 4–5 minutes on each side. Grill the red peppers until the skins have blackened and blistered, then carefully peel off the skin and cut lengthways into strips.

To serve, place the red mullet on individual serving plates, arranging the grilled red pepper strips at the side of the fish. Drizzle the green sauce generously around the fish.

SARDINAS AL HORNO CON SALSA DE TOMATE

BAKED SARDINES WITH FRESH TOMATO SAUCE

The Spanish are passionate about sardines and have some wonderful, uncomplicated ways of cooking them. One of the best ways to serve these nutritious little fish is with a fresh tomato sauce. Oven-baked with white wine, garlic and parsley, the sardines are delicious served with the puréed sweet, fresh tomatoes.

SERVES 4

12–16 sardines, depending on size, scaled and boned
4 tablespoons extra virgin olive oil
2 cloves garlic, crushed
2 tablespoons finely chopped flat-leaf parsley
150 ml/¼ pint dry white wine
freshly squeezed juice of ½ lemon
3 courgettes, sliced lengthways
sprigs of flat-leaf parsley and lemon wedges, to garnish

TOMATO SAUCE
3 tablespoons extra virgin olive oil
3 shallots, finely chopped
2 cloves garlic, finely chopped
1 kg/2 lb plum tomatoes, skinned, seeded and coarsely chopped
½ teaspoon sugar
freshly ground sea salt and black pepper

First make the tomato sauce. Place the olive oil in a saucepan and add the shallots and garlic. Sweat over a low heat for 4–5 minutes, until soft and translucent, but not coloured. Add the tomatoes, sugar and seasoning. Simmer over a moderate heat for about 15 minutes. Pour into a food processor or blender and process until smooth. Strain into a clean saucepan and adjust the seasoning.

Preheat the oven to 190°C/375°F/Gas Mark 5.

Pat the sardines dry on kitchen paper. Season lightly all over with salt and pepper, then brush generously with olive oil. Lay the sardines in a large ovenproof baking dish, then sprinkle the garlic and parsley on top. Pour over the white wine and lemon juice, then bake in the preheated oven for about 10 minutes.

Brush the courgettes lightly with olive oil, then place under a hot grill until lightly browned and tender.

To serve, arrange the grilled courgette slices on serving plates, then lay the baked sardines on top. Spoon the fresh tomato sauce around the sardines and garnish with lemon wedges and sprigs of flat-leaf parsley.

FRITTO MISTO DI MARE

DEEP-FRIED FISH

Fritto misto, a wonderful medley of crisp fish and shellfish, is a popular dish all along the Mediterranean coast of Italy, where there is a vast choice of fresh fish.

SERVES 4

12 large raw prawns, shelled and deveined, and tails left on
olive oil, for deep-frying
4 small red mullet, scaled, with liver left intact
4 small sardines, scaled
350 g/12 oz squid, cleaned and cut into rings, tentacles left whole
4 large lemons, cut into wedges

OLIVE OIL BATTER
250 g/8 oz plain flour
freshly ground sea salt and black pepper
4 tablespoons extra virgin olive oil
250 ml/8 fl oz warm water
4 egg whites

First prepare the batter. Sieve the flour into a large bowl and season lightly. Add the olive oil, mixing well, then gradually add sufficient warm water to give a smooth, fluid, lump-free consistency. Chill in the refrigerator for about 40 minutes. Beat the egg whites until they stand in stiff peaks, then gently fold into the chilled batter.

Heat the olive oil in a deep pan to approximately 180°C/350°F, or until a cube of bread browns in 30 seconds.

Coat all the fish and shellfish in the batter, then deep-fry in batches until crisp and golden. Cook the red mullet and sardines first, allowing 3–4 minutes, depending on their size. The prawns will take about 2 minutes, and the squid about 1½ minutes. Remove with a slotted spoon and drain on kitchen paper. Serve garnished with lemon wedges.

SALMONE AI FRUTTI DI MARE

SEARED SALMON WITH MUSSELS AND CLAMS

This delicious salmon dish takes only minutes to prepare and combines the wonderful flavours of both fish and shellfish enriched with garlic, parsley and white wine.

SERVES 4

4 salmon fillets, about 175 g/6 oz each, skinned and boned
freshly ground sea salt and black pepper
4 tablespoons extra virgin olive oil
4 cloves garlic, crushed
125 ml/4 fl oz dry white wine
125 ml/4 fl oz fish stock
4 tablespoons finely chopped parsley
12 mussels in their shells, scrubbed and beards removed
8 clams in their shells, scrubbed
lemon slices, to garnish

Pat the salmon fillets dry then season lightly. Warm the olive oil in a large frying pan, then add the garlic. Sauté over a low heat for about 2 minutes to infuse the oil, then remove the garlic from the pan with a slotted spoon and reserve.

Lay the salmon in the pan, and sear over a moderate heat for about 2 minutes on each side. Pour in the white wine, allowing it to bubble up, then add the fish stock, parsley and reserved garlic. Add the mussels and clams, cover and cook for 3–4 minutes until the fish is cooked through and the shellfish have been steamed open. Discard any shells that do not open.

Remove the salmon from the pan with a slotted spoon and place on individual serving plates. Arrange the mussels and clams around the fish. Reduce the juices over a fairly high heat for 1½–2 minutes, then pour over the salmon and shellfish. Garnish with lemon slices.

LOUP DE MER AU COULIS DE POIVRONS ROUGES

ROAST SEA BASS WITH LEMON PASTA AND RED PEPPER SAUCE

In this stunning dish, oven-roasted sea bass is served on a bed of lemon-scented tagliatelle and wilted spinach, dressed with a coulis of grilled red peppers, combining some of the vibrant flavours and colours that are so typical of Mediterranean cuisine.

Sea bass is a rich source of easily digested protein, low in saturated fat and a valuable source of omega-3 fatty acids – essential polyunsaturated oils that are beneficial to the health of the heart and circulation.

SERVES 4

4 sea bass fillets, about 175 g/6 oz each, scaled but with skin left on
freshly ground sea salt and black pepper
4 tablespoons extra virgin olive oil
500 g/1 lb spinach, tough stalks removed

RED PEPPER SAUCE
3 large red peppers, cored, seeded and halved
90 ml/3 fl oz extra virgin olive oil

LEMON PASTA
175 g/6 oz tagliatelle
4 tablespoons extra virgin olive oil
zest and freshly squeezed juice of ¹/₂ lemon
1 tablespoon chopped flat-leaf parsley

To make the red pepper sauce, grill the peppers, skin-side up, under a hot grill until the skins have blackened and blistered. Place in a plastic bag, seal and allow to cool. Peel off the skin. Reserve one of the grilled pepper halves, then place the remainder in a food processor or blender and process until smooth. With the motor still running, add sufficient olive oil to give a fluid consistency. Strain through a nylon sieve and season to taste.

Cut the reserved pepper into very small dice, then add to the sauce. Just before serving, warm very gently over a low heat, so that the sauce is just lukewarm.

To make the pasta, cook the tagliatelle in a large saucepan of lightly salted boiling water for 7–8 minutes, until it is al dente. Place the olive oil, lemon zest and juice in a small saucepan and warm over a very gentle heat to allow the flavours to infuse together. Remove from the heat, then add the chopped parsley to the oil. Just before serving, drain the pasta, then pour over the lemon-scented oil and toss well.

Preheat the oven to 200°C/400°F/Gas Mark 6.

Season the sea bass lightly all over with salt and pepper. Warm the olive oil in a large frying pan, then sear the sea bass briefly over a high heat for about 1 minute on each side. Transfer the seared fish, skin-side up, to a lightly oiled ovenproof dish, then roast in the preheated oven for 6 minutes. The sea bass skin should be quite crispy, but the flesh succulent and moist.

Rinse the spinach in cold water then place in a large saucepan. Season with salt and pepper, then cover and leave to wilt over a moderate heat for about 3 minutes.

To serve, spoon the wilted spinach on to individual serving plates, making a nest for the pasta. Spoon the lemon pasta on to the spinach, then lay the roast sea bass on top. Drizzle the red pepper sauce around the wilted spinach and serve at once.

ATUN A LA PLANCHA CON SALSA DE GAZPACHO

GRILLED TUNA WITH BRAISED FENNEL AND GAZPACHO SAUCE

Fresh tuna responds well to quick cooking, either grilling or searing over a high heat, and should be served pink and slightly rare so that the flesh remains juicy and moist.

SERVES 4

4 tuna steaks, about 2.5 cm/1 inch thick and 175 g/6 oz each, boned
2 cloves garlic, cut in half
2 tablespoons extra virgin olive oil

GAZPACHO SAUCE
1 large red pepper, halved, cored and seeded
4 large tomatoes, skinned, seeded and coarsely chopped
15 cm/6 inch piece of cucumber, peeled, seeded and coarsely chopped
1 clove garlic, crushed
pinch of sugar
2 tablespoons white wine vinegar
3 tablespoons extra virgin olive oil
1 tablespoon finely diced red pepper, cored and seeded
1 tablespoon finely diced cucumber
freshly ground sea salt and black pepper

BRAISED FENNEL
4 tablespoons extra virgin olive oil
4 small fennel bulbs, thickly sliced lengthways, feathery leaves reserved
125 ml/4 fl oz vegetable stock

To make the gazpacho sauce, grill the red pepper under a moderate grill until the skin has blackened and blistered. Place in a plastic bag, seal and leave to cool. When cool, peel off the skin.

Place the grilled pepper, tomatoes, cucumber, garlic, sugar and vinegar in a food processor or blender and process until smooth. With the motor still running, slowly add sufficient olive oil to give a light pouring consistency. Strain through a nylon sieve, season to taste, then add the raw red pepper and cucumber dice. Chill until ready to use.

To make the braised fennel, warm the olive oil in a large saucepan. Add the fennel and sweat over a very low heat for about 8 minutes. Pour in the vegetable stock and braise for a further 8–10 minutes, until the fennel is tender but not too soft and still al dente.

Rub each tuna steak with the cut sides of one of the garlic cloves, then brush lightly with olive oil.

Grill the tuna steaks under a hot grill for about 2 minutes on each side, so that the fish is still slightly pink inside. Over-cooking will make the tuna tough and dry.

Arrange the braised fennel on individual serving plates, then lay the grilled tuna on top. Drizzle the gazpacho sauce around the fennel and tuna. Finely chop the reserved fennel leaves and sprinkle over the tuna.

BEIGNETS DE SARDINES

BEIGNETS OF FRESH SARDINES

Fresh sardines are now widely available in supermarkets. They are easy to cook, and have the added bonus of being inexpensive, thoroughly delicious and highly nutritious. See page *xx* for instructions on boning them.

SERVES 4

12–16 sardines, scaled and boned
olive oil, for deep-frying
2 tablespoons finely chopped parsley
lemon wedges, to garnish

BATTER
125 g/4 oz plain flour
freshly ground sea salt and black pepper
2 tablespoons extra virgin olive oil
150 ml/¼ pint warm water
2 cloves garlic, crushed
2 egg whites, beaten until they stand in stiff peaks

First make the batter. Sieve the flour into a large bowl, then season. Mix the olive oil into the flour, then gradually add sufficient warm water to give a smooth, lump-free consistency. Mix in the garlic, then chill for about 1 hour, stirring from time to time. Just before cooking, gently fold the egg whites into the batter.

Pick out any stray bones from the sardines with a pair of tweezers. Heat the oil in a deep pan to 180°C/350°F, or until a cube of bread browns in 30 seconds. Dip the sardines in the batter, then deep-fry in hot oil for about 3 minutes, until crisp and golden. Remove with a slotted spoon and drain on kitchen paper. Arrange the sardines on a serving platter, sprinkle with parsley and garnish with lemon wedges.

SARDINE IN FOGLIE DI VITE

SARDINES IN VINE LEAVES

The Mediterranean custom of grilling sardines wrapped in vine leaves enhances the fish's lovely sweet flavour, preserving its moistness and infusing it with wonderful earthy aromas. Both sardines and red mullet are delicious cooked in this way, especially grilled over charcoal.

SERVES 4

12 vine leaves
12 sardines, scaled and boned
6 cloves garlic, crushed
2 tablespoons finely chopped fennel
1 tablespoon finely chopped shallot
1 tablespoon finely chopped fresh rosemary
4 tablespoons finely chopped parsley
freshly ground sea salt and black pepper
2–3 tablespoons extra virgin olive oil
lemon wedges and parsley sprigs, to garnish

If using preserved vine leaves, soak in water for about 30 minutes, changing the water once, to remove excess salt.

Remove any stray bones from the sardines with tweezers.

Mix together the garlic, fennel, onion, rosemary and parsley, then stuff the sardine cavities with this mixture. Season the fish lightly with salt and pepper.

Drain the vine leaves and pat dry on kitchen paper, then brush one side lightly with olive oil. Place a sardine on each oiled leaf and wrap up into a parcel, securing it with wooden cocktail sticks. Place under a hot grill and grill for 3–4 minutes on each side, depending on the size of the sardines. Serve with lemon wedges.

5
Poultry and Game

POULET AUX HERBES DE PROVENCE

CHICKEN WITH FRESH PROVENÇAL HERBS

This classic chicken dish is loved by everyone who savours its gorgeous aroma. Lightly sautéed in olive oil, the chicken is then infused with the fragrance of wonderful Provençal herbs, garlic and wine in a most delectable way.

SERVES 4

1.5 kg/3 lb free-range chicken, jointed into 8 pieces
freshly ground sea salt and black pepper
3 tablespoons extra virgin olive oil
4 cloves garlic, sliced lengthways
4 tablespoons finely chopped mixed fresh herbs such as flat-leaf parsley, thyme, rosemary, oregano and basil
300 ml/½ pint dry white wine
freshly squeezed juice of ½ lemon

Pat the chicken pieces dry on kitchen paper, then season all over with salt and pepper. Warm the olive oil in a large frying pan, then add the chicken pieces and sauté over a moderately high heat for 3–4 minutes, until golden brown all over.

Add the garlic and 3 tablespoons of the herbs to the chicken. Reduce the heat a little and continue to sauté for a further 2 minutes, stirring well so that the chicken is flavoured with the garlic and herbs. Pour in the white wine and bring to the boil, then cover and simmer gently for 25–30 minutes, until the chicken is moist and tender and the sauce has reduced to a light syrupy consistency.

Just before serving, pour the lemon juice over the chicken and sprinkle with the remaining fresh herbs.

POLLO ALLA MARSALA

CHICKEN BREASTS WITH WILD MUSHROOMS AND MARSALA

Wild mushrooms are more easily found than they used to be and really are an essential ingredient of this popular Italian dish. The succulent free-range chicken breasts, the tasty wild mushrooms and the sweet Marsala juices complement each other perfectly.
Chicken is high in protein, and an excellent source of B vitamins and the minerals iron and zinc. Skinless chicken breasts are low in fat, as most of the saturated fat in chicken is found in the skin.

SERVES 4

4 free-range chicken breasts, skinned and boned
freshly ground sea salt and black pepper
2 tablespoons plain flour
4 tablespoons extra virgin olive oil
3 cloves garlic, finely chopped
2 onions, finely chopped
350 g/12 oz mixed wild mushrooms, such as chanterelles, ceps,
oyster or shiitake, sliced
150 ml/1/4 pint Marsala
250 ml/8 fl oz chicken stock
2 tablespoons finely chopped flat-leaf parsley

Pat the chicken breasts dry, then season all over with salt and pepper. Dust the chicken breasts lightly with flour.
Warm the olive oil in a large frying pan, then sear the chicken over a moderately high heat for about $1^1/_2$ minutes on each side, until golden brown all over. Remove the chicken from the frying pan with a slotted spoon and place on a warm plate.

Pour off all but 1 tablespoon of the oil remaining in the pan, then add the garlic, onion and wild mushrooms. Sauté over a moderate heat for 3–4 minutes, without browning, then pour in the Marsala. Simmer until the Marsala is reduced by about half, then add the chicken stock.

Return the chicken breasts to the pan, together with any juices that have accumulated on the plate, then simmer over a moderate heat for 10–12 minutes, until the chicken breasts are cooked through and the sauce has reduced to a light, syrupy consistency.

Spoon the wild mushroom and Marsala sauce on to individual serving plates, then lay the chicken breasts on top. Sprinkle with finely chopped parsley and serve at once.

MAGRET DE CANARD AUX FIGUES, PARFUME A LA MADERE

BREAST OF DUCK WITH FRESH FIGS AND MADEIRA-SCENTED JUICES

This fashionable dish is much adored in France, and rightly so because fresh figs are yet another fruit that make a perfect companion for duck. The breast of duck is served quite simply, adorned by the figs and accompanied by nothing more than a light, Madeira-scented *jus*.

Duck contains high levels of saturated fat, but as much as two-thirds of the fat content is actually concentrated in the skin, so you can substantially reduce the amount of fat by removing the skin. The breasts themselves are the least fatty part of the bird. Like chicken, duck is a good source of protein, all the B vitamins and the minerals iron, potassium and zinc.

SERVES 4

4 duck breasts, skin and all traces of fat removed
freshly ground sea salt and black pepper
3 tablespoons extra virgin olive oil
90 ml/3 fl oz Madeira
350 ml/12 fl oz chicken stock
4 fresh figs

Pat the duck breasts dry on kitchen paper, then season on both sides with salt and pepper. Warm the olive oil in a large frying pan, then lay the seasoned breasts in the oil and sear over a high heat for about 1½ minutes on each side.

Preheat the oven to 190°C/375°F/Gas Mark 5.

Remove the duck breasts from the frying pan with a slotted spoon and place on a wire rack set over a large roasting dish. Prick the duck flesh all over with a fork – this enables the fat to be released and drained off. Roast for 8–10 minutes, until the flesh is browned on the outside, but still pink and tender inside.

Meanwhile, pour off all the fat remaining in the frying pan, then add the Madeira and stir to deglaze, allowing the wine to bubble up and absorb all the lovely cooking flavours. Pour in the chicken stock and boil over a high heat until reduced to a light, flavoured juice.

Place the figs in the oven for about 3 minutes, so that they are just gently softened and warmed through.

To serve, slice the duck breasts and arrange on warm serving plates. Pour the Madeira-scented juices around the duck breasts. Make 3 deep cuts in each fig and carefully open out into 6 segments, leaving the segments attached at the base of the fruit. Arrange the figs beside the duck breasts.

POLLO AL CHILINDRON

CHICKEN WITH SWEET RED PEPPERS AND TOMATOES

The chilindrón method of cooking both chicken and meat in a succulent sauce of sweet red peppers, onions, garlic and tomatoes is a speciality of the province of Aragon in North-east Spain. The sauce contains large amounts of the protective nutrients so typical of Mediterranean cuisine.

SERVES 4–6

1.5 kg/3 lb free-range chicken, jointed
freshly ground sea salt and black pepper
100 ml/3½ fl oz extra virgin olive oil
2 large Spanish onions, finely chopped
3 cloves garlic, finely chopped
3 large red peppers, cored, seeded and cut lengthways into strips
500 g/1 lb tomatoes, skinned, seeded and coarsely chopped
175 ml/6fl oz red wine
16 black olives, pitted

Pat the chicken pieces dry, then season lightly with salt and pepper. Warm half the olive oil in a large frying pan, then sauté the chicken pieces over a moderate heat until golden brown all over. Transfer the chicken with a slotted spoon to an ovenproof casserole dish.

Preheat the oven to 180°C/350°F/Gas Mark 4.

Pour off the oil remaining in the frying pan, wipe clean with kitchen paper, then pour the remaining olive oil into the pan. Add the chopped onion and sauté over a low heat until soft and translucent, but not coloured. Add the garlic and red peppers and continue to sauté until the peppers are soft. Now add the tomatoes and continue to cook until the tomatoes have softened, then pour in the red wine.

Season with salt and pepper, then pour the mixture over the chicken pieces.

Cover the casserole dish, then place in the preheated oven for about 30 minutes, until the chicken is tender and the sauce has reduced to a thick, rich red consistency. About 5 minutes before the end of the cooking time, add the black olives to the casserole to warm through. Serve the chicken and the sauce straight from the casserole, accompanied by plain rice or pasta.

PERDICES CON LENTEJAS

PARTRIDGE WITH LENTILS

Game birds are deliciously flavourful in a hearty casserole, partnered with lentils. Both partridge and pheasant are an ideal choice for this dish.
Game birds such as partridge have a very low saturated fat content and are a valuable source of protein, B vitamins and iron, while lentils are highly nutritious, rich in protein, fibre, B vitamins, iron and manganese.

SERVES 4

4 small partridges, cleaned and dressed
freshly ground sea salt and black pepper
3 tablespoons extra virgin olive oil
3 tablespoons sherry
2 bay leaves
1 sprig of rosemary

LENTILS
250 g/8 oz Puy lentils
900 ml/1½ pints game or chicken stock
1 large onion, peeled and finely chopped
2 cloves garlic, finely chopped
1 large carrot, finely chopped
1 celery stalk, finely chopped

Rinse the lentils under cold running water, discarding any discoloured ones. Place in a large saucepan, pour in the game stock and bring to the boil. Add the onion, garlic, carrot and celery, then simmer over a moderate heat for about 15 minutes, to soften the lentils. Drain and reserve the stock.

Season the partridges lightly all over with salt and

pepper. Warm the olive oil in a casserole dish large enough to hold the birds comfortably. Sauté the partridges over a moderate heat until golden brown all over. Pour in the sherry, allowing it to bubble up and absorb the juices, then add the lentils, bay leaves, rosemary and reserved stock. Cover the casserole and simmer over a low heat for about 45 minutes, until the partridges are tender.

POLLO AL AJILLO

SHERRY-SCENTED CHICKEN WITH THIRTY CLOVES OF GARLIC

A speciality of Andalucia, this beautiful chicken dish is laden with wonderful flavours. Don't be put off by the quantity of garlic used: when slow-cooked in this way the garlic becomes soft and creamy with a flavour that is quite subtle, and not at all strong.

The high level of garlic in this dish makes it especially nutritious. Garlic has for centuries been used as a folk remedy to cure a variety of ailments, and has long been recognized for its antibacterial and antiseptic properties. It is now known also to have powerful anticoagulant and antioxidant properties, highly beneficial to the heart and the immune system.

SERVES 4

1.5 kg/3 lb free-range chicken, jointed
freshly ground sea salt and black pepper
2 tablespoons plain flour
125 ml/4 fl oz extra virgin olive oil
3 heads of garlic, split into about 30 cloves, peeled but left whole
200 ml/7 fl oz dry sherry
2–3 bay leaves
dried thyme, to sprinkle

Pat the chicken pieces dry on kitchen paper, then season all over with salt and pepper. Dust the chicken lightly with flour.

Warm the olive oil in a large, heavy-based frying pan or casserole dish, then add the chicken pieces and sauté over a moderate heat, turning from time to time, until golden brown. Remove the chicken with a slotted spoon and reserve.

Add the 30 cloves of garlic to the oil remaining in the frying pan and sauté gently for about 2 minutes to soften. Pour in the sherry, allowing it to bubble up and absorb all the cooking juices, then return the chicken pieces to the pan. Add the bay leaf, cover and simmer over a moderate heat for about 35 minutes, until the chicken is tender and the juices have reduced to a light syrupy consistency. Sprinkle lightly with thyme and serve at once, giving each person about 7 of the garlic cloves.

POLLO CON PASAS Y PINONES

CHICKEN WITH RAISINS AND PINE NUTS

Pine nuts are very popular in Spain and appear in many regional dishes. In this delicious Catalan recipe, the crunchy texture of toasted pine nuts marries beautifully with the sweet, sherry-scented chicken and plump raisins. Pine nuts are a rich source of vitamin E, thought to be the most effective antioxidant nutrient, vital to the health of the heart, circulation and immune system. Vitamin E can also help to prevent premature ageing, retarding cellular damage due to oxidation.

SERVES 4

2 tablespoons raisins
200 ml/7 fl oz dry sherry
1.5 kg/3 lb free-range chicken, jointed
freshly ground sea salt and black pepper
2 tablespoons plain flour
100 ml/3½ fl oz extra virgin olive oil
1 large onion, finely chopped
1 red pepper, cored, seeded and finely chopped
2 cloves garlic, finely chopped
125 g/4 oz pine nuts, very lightly toasted
1 tablespoon finely chopped flat-leaf parsley

Cover the raisins with the sherry and leave to soak for about 1 hour, to soften.

Pat the chicken pieces dry and season all over with salt and pepper. Toss the chicken pieces lightly in the flour.

Warm the olive oil in a large heavy-based frying pan or casserole dish, then add the chicken pieces. Sauté over a moderate heat, turning from time to time, until golden brown, then remove from the pan with a slotted spoon and reserve. Add the onion, red pepper, garlic and raisins to the pan and sauté over a gentle heat for 4–5 minutes until soft but not coloured.

Pour the sherry on to the vegetables and raisins, allowing it to bubble up and absorb the cooking juices, then return the chicken pieces to the pan. Lower the heat to simmering point, cover and simmer gently for about 30 minutes, until the chicken is tender, and the juices have reduced to a light, syrupy sauce. If necessary, add a little water or chicken stock to prevent the chicken from sticking.

Add the toasted pine nuts to the chicken, sprinkle with parsley and serve at once.

POULET A LA VIEILLE NICOISE

OLD NIÇOISE-STYLE CHICKEN

The traditional old Niçoise style of cooking is one of the finest in the world, creating wonderful marriages of flavour with fresh ingredients, cooked simply but with style. Indeed, much of modern cuisine takes its roots from the partnership of flavours created in this style. In this dish, chicken is cooked with a beautiful, fresh-flavoured sauce of tomatoes, courgettes, sweet peppers, black olives and basil, with a hint of red wine. Red wine is a healthy cooking medium for vegetables and protein, adding antioxidant nutrients.

SERVES 4

1.5 kg/3 lb free-range chicken, jointed into 8 pieces
freshly ground sea salt and black pepper
2 tablespoons plain flour
4 tablespoons extra virgin olive oil
2 shallots, finely chopped
1 red and 1 yellow pepper, cored, seeded and cut lengthways into strips
2 courgettes, sliced into rings
3 cloves garlic, finely chopped
1 kg/2 lb tomatoes, skinned, seeded and coarsely chopped
300 ml/¹/₂ pint red wine
60 g/2 oz black olives
generous handful of basil leaves, coarsely torn

Pat the chicken pieces dry on kitchen paper, then season with salt and pepper. Dust the chicken pieces lightly with flour.

Warm 2 tablespoons of the oil in a large frying pan or casserole dish, then add the chicken pieces and sauté over a moderate heat until lightly browned all over. Remove the chicken from the pan with a slotted spoon and reserve.

Add the shallots, peppers, courgettes and garlic, together with the remaining 2 tablespoons of olive oil. Sauté over a moderate heat until soft, then add the tomatoes and red wine. Bring slowly to the boil, stirring from time to time, then return the chicken pieces to the pan, cover and simmer over a gentle heat for about 30 minutes, until the chicken is cooked and the sauce is thick and mellow. Add the black olives to the pan during the final minutes of cooking time. Sprinkle generously with fresh basil leaves and serve piping hot.

POLLO ALLA ROMANA

SAUTÉED CHICKEN WITH TRIO OF PEPPERS

Sweet red, yellow and green peppers add great colour and flavour to this mouthwatering Roman-style chicken dish. High levels of vitamin C and carotenoid nutrients are supplied by the peppers and tomatoes in this dish.

SERVES 4

1.5 kg / 3 lb free-range chicken, jointed into 8 pieces
freshly ground sea salt and black pepper
2 tablespoons plain flour
100 ml / 3½ fl oz extra virgin olive oil
2 large onions, finely chopped
4 cloves garlic, finely chopped
2 large red peppers, cored, seeded and sliced lengthways into 6 pieces
1 large yellow pepper, cored, seeded and sliced lengthways into 6 pieces
1 large green pepper, cored, seeded and sliced lengthways into 6 pieces
125 g / 4 oz mushrooms, sliced
350 g / 12 oz tomatoes, skinned, seeded and coarsely chopped
300 ml / ½ pint dry white wine
450 ml / ¾ pint chicken stock
2 generous handfuls of basil leaves, coarsely torn
1 tablespoon finely chopped rosemary leaves
2 tablespoons finely chopped parsley

Pat the chicken dry on kitchen paper and season lightly all over with salt and pepper. Dust the chicken lightly with flour.

Warm half the olive oil in a large casserole dish, then sauté the chicken pieces over a moderate heat until golden brown all over. Remove the chicken from the casserole with a slotted spoon and reserve.

Preheat the oven to 180°C/350°F/Gas Mark 4.

Pour the remaining olive oil into the casserole dish, then add the onions, garlic, peppers and mushrooms. Cover and sweat over a low heat for 3–4 minutes until soft and translucent, then add the chopped tomatoes. Return the chicken pieces to the casserole dish, then pour in the white wine and chicken stock. Bring to the boil, then add half the basil leaves, the rosemary and the parsley. Cover and place in the preheated oven for about 25 minutes, until the chicken is cooked.

Just before serving, sprinkle the remaining basil over the chicken and vegetables, and serve hot, with pasta or rice.

DELICE DE FAISAN AUX FRUITS DE LA FORET

BREAST OF PHEASANT WITH FOREST FRUITS AND RUBY SAUCE

A sweet and sour sauce made with soft fruit is an ideal companion for game birds. With a low saturated fat content, and very little fatty tissue, game birds such as pheasant make a healthy alternative to red meat. Rich in protein, pheasant provides substantial amounts of the B complex group of vitamins and iron too, while the fruit has a high concentration of vitamin C.

SERVES 4

4 pheasant breasts
freshly ground sea salt and black pepper
4 tablespoons extra virgin olive oil

FOREST FRUITS AND RUBY SAUCE
125 g/4 oz blackcurrants
125 g/4 oz redcurrants
125 g/4 oz blackberries
2 tablespoons brown sugar
125 ml/4 fl oz water
150 ml/¼ pint ruby port
4 tablespoons red wine vinegar
300 ml/½ pint game stock

To make the sauce, rinse the fruit well. Place the brown sugar and water in a saucepan over a moderate heat, stirring well until the sugar has dissolved. Add the fruit and poach gently for 4–5 minutes until tender, but not too soft. Remove from the heat and set aside.

Pat the pheasant breasts dry on kitchen paper, then season

all over with salt and pepper. Warm the olive oil in a large frying pan, then sauté the breasts over a moderate heat for 4–5 minutes on each side, until golden brown and springy to the touch. Remove from the pan and keep warm.

Pour off all the oil remaining in the pan, then stir in the ruby port to deglaze, allowing the port to bubble up and absorb the juices. Add the vinegar and game stock, then boil over a moderate heat until reduced by about half. Add the poached fruit to the stock and warm through. Adjust the seasoning.

To serve, slice each pheasant breast lengthways into 3 or 4 slices, then arrange on individual serving plates. Spoon the fruit and juices around the pheasant and serve at once.

SALADE DE POULET A LA MANGUE, VINAIGRETTE A L'ORANGE ET A LA MENTHE

WARM SALAD OF CHICKEN AND MANGO WITH MINTED ORANGE DRESSING

Mangoes are very popular in France, although not a native fruit. This colourful salad makes an ideal summer lunch, the flavour of the fruit blending well with the honey-glazed chicken breasts and the fragrant vinaigrette.

Deeply pigmented salad leaves such as rocket, radicchio and spinach contain high levels of beta-carotene, providing as well valuable amounts of vitamin C, and the minerals folate, iron and potassium. The beta-carotene content of the salad is substantially increased by the mango, one of the richest fruit sources of this vitally important nutrient.

SERVES 4

4 free-range chicken breasts, skinned and boned
freshly ground sea salt and black pepper
1 tablespoon clear honey
4 ripe mangoes, peeled, stoned and cut into strips
4 generous handfuls of mixed pink and green salad leaves, such
as rocket, radicchio and spinach

MINTED ORANGE DRESSING
175 ml/6 fl oz extra virgin olive oil
1 tablespoon balsamic vinegar
1 tablespoon freshly squeezed orange juice
½ teaspoon Dijon mustard
½ teaspoon clear honey
finely grated zest of ½ orange
1 tablespoon finely chopped mint leaves

Pat the chicken breasts dry on kitchen paper, then season on both sides with salt and pepper. Grill the chicken breasts under a moderate grill for 8–10 minutes, depending on their size, until firm and springy to the touch. About half-way through the cooking time, smear the honey all over the chicken skin, so that the breasts are glazed to a rich golden brown colour when cooked.

To prepare the dressing, whisk the olive oil and vinegar together until thoroughly emulsified. Whisk in the orange juice, Dijon mustard, honey, grated orange zest and chopped fresh mint, blending all the ingredients together thoroughly, then season to taste.

Add the mango to the salad leaves, then arrange on individual serving plates. Slice the chicken breasts and arrange over the salad leaves. Drizzle the minted orange dressing over the salad and serve at once, while the chicken is still warm.

POLLO ALLA CACCIATORE

HUNTER'S STYLE CHICKEN CASSEROLE WITH MUSHROOMS, TOMATOES, GARLIC AND ROSEMARY

This is one of those lovely rustic Italian casseroles where everything is just thrown in haphazardly and as if by magic turns into a beautiful meal, rich in wonderful flavours. Although hard to believe, red wine is actually a healthy cooking medium, providing antioxidant nutrients derived from the deeply pigmented red skin of the grapes.

SERVES 4

1.5 kg/3 lb free-range chicken, jointed
freshly ground sea salt and black pepper
2 tablespoons plain flour
4 tablespoons extra virgin olive oil
2 large red onions, finely chopped
4 cloves garlic, finely chopped
2 courgettes, sliced
350 g/12 oz mixed wild mushrooms such as chanterelles, ceps,
oyster or shiitake, sliced
1 kg/2 lb plum tomatoes, skinned, seeded and coarsely chopped
1 teaspoon sugar
2 tablespoons balsamic vinegar
300 ml/1/2 pint red wine
125 ml/4 fl oz chicken stock
2 sprigs of rosemary

Pat the chicken dry on kitchen paper, then season all over with salt and pepper. Dust the chicken pieces lightly with flour. Warm the olive oil in a large casserole dish, then sear the chicken pieces over a moderately high heat until golden brown all over. Remove the chicken pieces with a slotted spoon and place on a warm plate.

Pour off all but 1 tablespoon of the oil remaining in the casserole dish, then add the red onion, garlic, courgettes and mushrooms. Sauté over a low heat for about 3 minutes, to soften, then add the tomatoes, sugar, vinegar, red wine, chicken stock and rosemary. Bring to the boil and cook over a moderate heat for about 2 minutes, stirring well.

Preheat the oven to 180°C/350°F/Gas Mark 4.

Return the chicken pieces to the casserole dish, together with any juices that have accumulated on the plate, then cover and cook in the preheated oven for 35–40 minutes, until the chicken is tender and moist and the sauce is rich and thick.

POLLO A LA VALENCIANA

VALENCIAN-STYLE CHICKEN WITH ORANGES AND BLACK OLIVES

With all those beautiful lush orange groves, it's not surprising that Valencia and its surrounding areas use oranges as a main ingredient in many of their sweet and savoury dishes. In this delicious recipe, the rich orange flavours are in perfect harmony with the succulent pan-fried chicken, glistening black olives and sherry-scented juices.

SERVES 4

4 large oranges
1.5 kg/3 lb free-range chicken, jointed into 8 pieces
freshly ground sea salt and black pepper
2 tablespoons plain flour
3 tablespoons extra virgin olive oil
175 ml/6 fl oz dry sherry
200 ml/7 fl oz chicken stock
2 cloves garlic, crushed
1 sprig of thyme
20 black olives, stoned
2 tablespoons finely chopped flat-leaf parsley

Pare the zest from 2 of the oranges and cut into fine julienne strips. Blanch in boiling water for about 5 minutes, then drain. Peel the 2 remaining oranges and remove the white pith from all the oranges. Carefully cut the 4 oranges into segments, discarding the membrane.

Pat the chicken dry on kitchen paper, then season with salt and pepper. Dust the chicken pieces lightly with flour. Warm the olive oil in a large frying pan, then sear the chicken pieces over a moderately high heat for 3–4 minutes, until golden brown all over.

Pour in the sherry, allowing it to bubble up and absorb all the lovely cooking juices. Reduce the sherry by about half, then add the chicken stock, garlic, thyme and orange strips.

Cover and simmer gently for about 10 minutes, then add the orange segments and black olives to the pan. Simmer for a further 10 minutes, until the chicken is tender and moist and the sauce is shiny and glistening. Sprinkle with chopped fresh parsley and serve at once.

POLLO AL LIMONE

LEMON-SCENTED CHICKEN WITH GARLIC AND PARSLEY

Lemon, olive oil and honey make a great marinade for chicken, and in this lovely Italian recipe the grilled lemon-scented breasts are finished off by spiking with a flavouring of lemon zest, garlic and parsley.

SERVES 4

4 free-range chicken breasts, skinned and boned

MARINADE
freshly squeezed juice of 1 lemon
4 tablespoons extra virgin olive oil
2 teaspoons clear honey
1 teaspoon coarsely ground black pepper
2 twists freshly ground sea salt

GREMOLATA
finely grated zest of 1 lemon
3 cloves garlic, crushed
4 tablespoons finely chopped parsley

Combine all the ingredients for the marinade in a large bowl and mix well until thoroughly emulsified. Add the chicken breasts, turning to coat completely, then leave to marinate in the refrigerator for several hours, turning from time to time.

Remove the chicken from the marinade and grill under a medium-hot grill for 6–8 minutes on each side, until golden brown and firm and springy to the touch.

Prepare the gremolata by mixing the finely grated lemon zest, garlic and finely chopped parsley together. Sprinkle the gremolata lightly over the chicken breasts and serve at once.

6
Pasta and Rice

RIGATONI CON I BROCCOLI

RIGATONI WITH BROCCOLI, ANCHOVIES AND BLACK OLIVES

Tubular-shaped pasta is perfect for a chunky sauce such as this, with crunchy, fresh-tasting broccoli florets. The flavours and colours are stunning in this dish, with the broccoli, olives and pasta blending together beautifully.

SERVES 4

12 anchovy fillets in olive oil, drained (optional)
milk for soaking
150 g/5 oz good quality black olives, pitted and coarsely chopped
2 cloves garlic, crushed
175 ml/6 fl oz extra virgin olive oil
2 tablespoons finely chopped flat-leaf parsley
500 g/1 lb rigatoni
625 g/1 lb 4oz broccoli, trimmed and divided into florets
freshly ground sea salt and black pepper

Soak the anchovies in milk for about 10 minutes, to remove excess saltiness. Pat the anchovies dry on kitchen paper, then cut into pieces and mix with the olives and garlic.

Place the olive oil in a saucepan set over a low heat, then add the anchovy mixture and the parsley. Warm through, then remove from the heat and leave the flavours to mingle.

Bring a large saucepan of lightly salted water to the boil, then stir in the rigatoni. Cook the pasta over a fairly high heat for 8–10 minutes, until it is al dente.

Steam the broccoli very briefly for no more than 1-1½ minutes, so that it is just tender, but still al dente.

Drain the pasta and place in a warm bowl, then pour over the olive oil mixture. Toss well, then add the broccoli florets and mix lightly into the pasta. Season and serve at once.

PASTA CON ALICI E AGLIO

PASTA WITH ANCHOVIES AND GARLIC

Anchovies are a popular ingredient for pasta sauces in Italy, and having tried many, this is certainly the most delicious anchovy pasta dish I have ever tasted.

SERVES 4

16 anchovy fillets in olive oil, drained
milk, for soaking
2 cloves garlic, crushed
2 tablespoons finely chopped flat-leaf parsley
1 tablespoon freshly squeezed lemon juice
150 ml/$^1/_2$ pint extra virgin olive oil
freshly ground sea salt and black pepper
4 red peppers
500 g/1 lb spaghetti or linguine
4 sprigs of flat-leaf parsley, to garnish

Soak the anchovies in milk for about 10 minutes, then drain and dry on kitchen paper. Pound the anchovies, garlic and parsley to a smooth paste, using a pestle and mortar, then gradually incorporate the lemon juice. Add the olive oil in a thin stream, mixing well until thoroughly emulsified, then season with black pepper. Preheat the oven to 180°C/350°F/Gas Mark 4.

Roast the red peppers until the skin has blackened and blistered. Place the peppers in a plastic bag and seal. When cool, peel off the skin, core and seed the peppers, then cut into strips and keep warm.

Bring a large saucepan of lightly salted water to the boil, then stir in the pasta. Cook for 7–8 minutes, until the pasta is al dente. Drain and transfer to a large bowl. Add the anchovy sauce, and toss well. Serve in individual bowls, with pepper strips on top. Garnish with parsley.

RISOTTO AI TRE FUNGHI

RISOTTO WITH A TRIO OF MUSHROOM FLAVOURS

All varieties of mushrooms are adored by the Italians, and this wonderfully rich, creamy risotto, laden with mushroom flavours, is no exception. Shiitake and oyster mushrooms are widely available in supermarkets, with chanterelles available from good delicatessens in spring and early summer. If you are unable to find fresh chanterelles, dried ones will make a good substitute.
Risotto rice is another great source of complex carbohydrates, slowly absorbed by the body and providing a steady release of energy into the bloodstream.

SERVES 4–6

100 ml/3½ fl oz extra virgin olive oil
175 g/6 oz oyster mushrooms, thickly sliced
175 g/6 oz shiitake mushrooms, thickly sliced
2 cloves garlic, finely chopped
125 g/4 oz chanterelles, coarsely chopped
freshly squeezed juice of ½ lemon
3 tablespoons finely chopped flat-leaf parsley
freshly ground sea salt and black pepper

RISOTTO
2 tablespoons extra virgin olive oil
2 shallots, finely chopped
250 g/8 oz arborio rice
90 ml/3 fl oz dry white wine
1 bay leaf
900 ml/1½ pints hot chicken stock
90 g/3 oz freshly grated Parmesan cheese

Warm the olive oil in a large saucepan, then add the oyster and shiitake mushrooms and the garlic. Sauté over a moderate heat for 3–4 minutes, until soft, then add the chanterelles. Continue to cook for a further 2–3 minutes, then add the lemon juice, 2 tablespoons of parsley and seasoning. Remove from the heat and set aside.

To make the risotto, warm the olive oil in a large, heavy-based saucepan, then add the finely chopped shallots. Sweat over a low heat until soft and translucent, but not coloured. Stir in the arborio rice and cook for 2–3 minutes until translucent. Pour in the white wine, add the bay leaf and reduce until all the wine has been absorbed, stirring continuously.

Begin adding the chicken stock over a moderate heat, one ladleful at a time and stirring well after each addition, until the stock has been absorbed by the rice. Carry on adding more stock as each ladleful is absorbed. After about 15–20 minutes, the rice should be tender, but still al dente, with all the stock absorbed.

Remove from the heat, then stir in the mushrooms and grated Parmesan. Stir for a couple of minutes until the cheese has melted, then serve the risotto in warm bowls, sprinkled with the remaining parsley.

RISOTTO DI CAPESANTE BAIA DI NAPOLI

BAY OF NAPLES RISOTTO OF SCALLOPS

This heavenly, champagne-scented risotto, with beautiful grilled scallops and a melting coral and chervil cream, is laden with the flavour of the sea.
Scallops are an excellent source of protein and have a low saturated fat content. Crème fraîche has a lower butterfat content than double cream, but it is still high in saturated fat, so use sparingly.

SERVES 4

12 scallops with corals, shelled
100 ml / 3½ fl oz fish stock
1½ tablespoons crème fraîche
freshly ground sea salt and black pepper
2 tablespoons finely chopped fresh chervil

CHAMPAGNE RISOTTO
2 tablespoons extra virgin olive oil
2 shallots, finely chopped
250 g / 8 oz arborio rice
150 ml / ¼ pint champagne or dry white wine
750 ml / 1¼ pints hot fish stock
sprigs of fresh chervil, to garnish

Rinse the scallops under cold running water and carefully remove the corals. Heat the fish stock to boiling point, then reduce the heat, add the corals and poach over a moderate heat for about 3 minutes. Remove from the heat and leave to cool in the stock.

To make the coral and chervil cream, drain the corals when cool and pat dry. Pound in a mortar, adding 1½–2 tablespoons of crème fraîche, until it has a smooth, creamy consistency. Season with salt and pepper, then mix in the chopped chervil.

To make the risotto, warm the oil in a large heavy-based saucepan, then add the shallots. Sweat over a low heat for 4–5 minutes, until soft and translucent, but not coloured. Stir in the arborio rice and cook for a further 2–3 minutes, until translucent. Pour in the champagne and simmer over a moderate heat, stirring all the time, until all the liquid has evaporated and the champagne flavours have been absorbed by the rice.

Gradually add the fish stock, one ladleful at a time and stirring well after each addition, until the stock has been absorbed by the rice. Continue to add more stock as each ladleful is absorbed. After about 15–20 minutes, the rice should be tender, but still al dente, with all the stock absorbed. Remove from the heat, then stir in the coral and chervil cream.

Grill the scallops under a hot grill for about 1 minute on each side. Serve the risotto in warm serving bowls, with the grilled scallops on top, allowing 3 scallops per person. Garnish with sprigs of fresh chervil.

SPAGHETTI DI NAPOLI

NEAPOLITAN-STYLE SPAGHETTI WITH OLIVE OIL, GARLIC, TOMATOES AND CHILLI PEPPER

The beautiful Bay of Naples is home to some of the most simple and delicious of Italian food. Fabled for its almost austere lack of meat and classic use of pasta, tomatoes, olive oil and garlic, Neapolitan cuisine has mastered the art of making simple ingredients taste absolutely superb.

SERVES 4

500 g/1 lb spaghetti
100 ml/3½ fl oz extra virgin olive oil
3 cloves garlic, finely chopped
1 small chilli pepper, seeded and finely chopped
1 kg/2 lb plum tomatoes, skinned, seeded and pulped
1 tablespoon tomato purée
freshly ground sea salt and black pepper
4 tablespoons finely chopped parsley

Bring a large saucepan of lightly salted water to the boil, then stir in the spaghetti. Cook the pasta over a fairly high heat for 7–8 minutes, until it is al dente.

While the spaghetti is cooking, warm the olive oil in a saucepan, then add the finely chopped garlic and chilli pepper. Sauté over a gentle heat, without allowing to colour, then stir in the pulped tomatoes and tomato purée. Cook over a gentle heat for about 6 minutes, until the pasta is ready.

Drain the spaghetti, then transfer to a warm bowl. Pour the sauce over the pasta and toss well. Season to taste with salt and pepper, then sprinkle with finely chopped parsley.

PENNE ALLA MOZZARELLA

PENNE WITH MOZZARELLA, TOMATOES AND BASIL

Another classic Neapolitan pasta dish, making simple yet superb use of that perfect tomato and basil partnership, with the addition of one of Italy's favourite cheeses. Soft cheeses such as mozzarella have a lower saturated fat content than firm-textured cheeses such as Cheddar or Parmesan.

SERVES 4

4 tablespoons extra virgin olive oil
2 onions, finely chopped
1 clove garlic, finely chopped
500 g / 1 lb plum tomatoes, skinned, seeded and coarsely chopped
freshly ground sea salt and black pepper
generous handful of basil leaves, coarsely torn
425 g / 14 oz penne
175 g / 6 oz mozzarella cheese, cubed

Warm the olive oil in a large saucepan, then add the onions and garlic. Sweat over a low heat until soft and translucent, but not coloured. Add the tomatoes and cook for a further 5–6 minutes, until reduced to a soft pulp. Season to taste with salt and pepper, then stir in two-thirds of the basil leaves.

Bring a large saucepan of lightly salted water to the boil, then stir in the penne. Cook the pasta over a fairly high heat for 8–10 minutes, until it is al dente.

Drain the penne and transfer to a warm serving bowl. Pour over the tomato and basil sauce, and toss well. Mix the mozzarella into the pasta. Serve at once in individual bowls, sprinkled with the remaining basil leaves.

CAPELLI D'ANGELO AL GRANCHIO E LIMONE

ANGEL'S HAIR PASTA WITH CRAB MEAT AND LEMON

Angel's hair is one of the finest pastas and its delicate, fragile texture requires only a very light sauce. This wonderful marriage of crab meat, lemon, olive oil, garlic and parsley is suberb with it.

SERVES 4

5 tablespoons extra virgin olive oil
1 clove garlic, crushed
350 g/12 oz fresh white crab meat
grated zest and freshly squeezed juice of 2 large lemons
2 tablespoons chopped flat-leaf parsley
freshly ground sea salt and black pepper
500 g/1 lb angel's hair pasta

Warm the olive oil in a small saucepan and add the garlic. Cook over a low heat until the garlic is soft but not coloured. Add the crab meat and warm over a low heat for just 1 minute, then stir in the lemon zest, lemon juice and parsley. Remove from the heat and season with salt and pepper.

Bring a large saucepan of lightly salted water to the boil, then stir in the angel's hair pasta. Cook the pasta for about 2 minutes, until it is al dente. Drain thoroughly, then add the pasta to the crab and lemon sauce and toss well. Serve at once.

SPAGHETTI AL LIMONE

SPAGHETTI WITH LEMON, PINE NUTS AND BASIL

The refreshing, natural flavours of lemon, toasted pine nuts and fresh basil complement each other beautifully in this simple pasta dish. Pine nuts contain high levels of vitamin E, one of the most potent antioxidant nutrients.

SERVES 4

100 g/3½ oz pine nuts
2 cloves garlic, crushed
100 ml/3½ fl oz extra virgin olive oil
freshly squeezed juice of 2 lemons
finely grated zest of 1 lemon
500 g/1 lb spaghetti
2 generous handfuls of basil leaves
60 g/2 oz freshly grated Parmesan cheese

Place the pine nuts in a dry saucepan and lightly toast over a moderate heat until golden.

Place the garlic and olive oil in a small saucepan and warm over a very low heat so that the garlic is softened and flavours the oil, without browning.

Crush the pine nuts lightly then add the lemon juice and zest. Add the garlic and oil, mixing together well.

Bring a large saucepan of lightly salted water to the boil, then stir in the spaghetti. Cook the pasta over a fairly high heat for 7–8 minutes until it is al dente. Drain the spaghetti and place in a large, warm bowl. Add the lemon and pine nut sauce, mixing well. Add the basil leaves to the spaghetti, and toss well. Serve in individual bowls, sprinkled with freshly grated Parmesan.

RISOTTO DI COZZE E FINOCCHI AL ZAFFERANO

SAFFRON RISOTTO WITH MUSSELS AND FENNEL

Mussels and fennel complement each other beautifully, and make a delicious addition to this golden, saffron-scented risotto.
Low in saturated fat, high in protein and rich in the minerals iron, iodine and zinc, mussels make an ideal partner for the complex carbohydrates supplied by the rice.

SERVES 4

1 kg/2 lb mussels in their shells, scrubbed and beards removed
200 ml/7 fl oz dry white wine
125 ml/4 fl oz water
2 shallots, finely chopped
1 clove garlic, crushed
750 ml/1¼ pints hot fish stock

RISOTTO
2 tablespoons extra virgin olive oil
1 fennel bulb, sliced lengthways into fine julienne strips, feathery leaves reserved
2 shallots, finely chopped
1 clove garlic, finely chopped
250 g/8 oz arborio rice
¼ teaspoon saffron threads

Discard any mussel shells that are not tightly closed. Place the dry white wine, water, shallots, and garlic in a saucepan and bring to the boil. Add the mussels, cover and boil over a fairly high heat until all the shells have opened. Discard any that fail to open. Drain the mussels, reserving all the juices. Strain the cooking juices and add to the fish stock.

To make the risotto, warm the olive oil in a large sauce-pan and add the fennel, shallots and garlic. Sweat over a low heat until soft and translucent, but not coloured.

Stir in the arborio rice and cook for 2-3 minutes until translucent. Begin adding the fish stock to the rice over a moderate heat, one ladleful at a time and stirring well after each addition, until the stock has been absorbed by the rice. Carry on adding more stock as each ladleful is absorbed. After about 15–20 minutes the rice should be tender, but still al dente, with all the stock absorbed.

Add the saffron to the risotto and stir through until all the saffron has dissolved. Leave 12 of the mussels in their shells, but shell the remainder and add to the risotto.

Serve the risotto in warm bowls, garnishing each bowl with 3 mussels in their shells. Finely chop the reserved fennel leaves and sprinkle over the risotto.

SPAGHETTI CON SARDINE

SPAGHETTI WITH FRESH SARDINES, FENNEL AND TOMATOES

There really is no substitute for fresh sardines, and while canned ones make a handy store-cupboard alternative, there is no comparison with the flavour of fresh ones. The sweetness of the sardines marries beautifully with the aromatic flavour of the fennel, whilst tomatoes of course make a perfect partner for sardines. Sardines are a valuable source of protein, low in saturated fat and one of the richest sources of essential omega-3 fatty acids, a healthy type of polyunsatureated fat.

SERVES 4

750 g/1½ lb sardines, scaled and boned
freshly ground sea salt and black pepper
2 tablespoons plain flour
6 anchovy fillets in olive oil, drained
milk, for soaking
6 tablespoons extra virgin olive oil
1 large onion, finely chopped
1 fennel bulb, cut lengthways into julienne strips, feathery leaves reserved
2 cloves garlic, finely chopped
1 kg/2 lb plum tomatoes, skinned, seeded and coarsely chopped
2 tablespoons finely chopped flat-leaf parsley
175 ml/6 fl oz dry white wine
500 g/1 lb spaghetti

Cut each of the sardines into 2 fillets, and carefully remove any remaining bones with tweezers. Season lightly all over, then dust lightly with flour.

Soak the anchovies in milk for about 10 minutes, to

reduce their saltiness. Drain, pat dry on kitchen paper and cut into pieces. Warm 3 tablespoons of olive oil in a large frying pan, then add the onion, fennel, garlic and anchovies. Sauté over a low heat for about 5 minutes, until soft and glistening. Add the tomatoes, parsley and wine, and simmer over a moderate heat until reduced to a thick, pulpy sauce. Season to taste.

Warm the remaining oil in a separate frying pan, then sauté the sardines briefly over a moderate heat until golden.

Bring a large saucepan of lightly salted water to the boil, then stir in the spaghetti. Cook the pasta over a fairly high heat for 7–8 minutes, until the spaghetti is al dente. Drain the pasta and transfer to a large, warm bowl. Pour over the tomato and fennel sauce and toss well.

Arrange the sardine fillets in a circle over the pasta. Finely chop the reserved fennel leaves and sprinkle over the sardines to garnish.

PENNE AL TONNO

PENNE WITH FRESH TUNA, BLACK OLIVES AND
TOMATOES

Fresh tuna is becoming more widely available as we become
increasingly aware of the health advantages of eating oily
fresh fish. This gorgeous pasta dish, with such a wonderful
variety of Mediterranean flavours, is an encouragement
to buy the real thing, rather than opening a can for
convenience.

SERVES 4

freshly ground sea salt and black pepper
2 × 250 g / 8 oz tuna steaks
4 tablespoons extra virgin olive oil
1 onion, finely chopped
2 cloves garlic, finely chopped
1 kg / 2 lb plum tomatoes, skinned, seeded and coarsely chopped
125 ml / 4 fl oz dry white wine
2 tablespoons capers, drained
90 g / 3 oz good quality black olives, pitted and halved
500 g / 1 lb penne
generous handful of basil leaves, coarsely torn

Season the tuna lightly all over. Warm 2 tablespoons of olive
oil in a large frying pan, then sear the tuna over a fairly high
heat for 1-1½ minutes on each side. Remove from the pan
and allow to cool, then flake the tuna flesh with a fork.

Warm the remaining oil in a clean pan and add the onion
and garlic. Sauté over a low heat until soft and translucent,
but not coloured, then add the tomatoes and white wine.
Simmer over a moderate heat for about 15 minutes, until
reduced to a thick, pulpy sauce. Add the capers, black olives
and tuna to the sauce and season to taste.

Bring a large saucepan of lightly salted water to the boil, then stir in the penne. Cook the pasta over a fairly high heat for 8–10 minutes, until it is al dente. Drain the pasta and transfer to a large warm bowl. Pour over the tuna sauce and toss well. Sprinkle generously with fresh basil just before serving.

RISOTTO NERO CON SPAGHETTI DI CALAMARI

BLACK RISOTTO WITH SQUID SPAGHETTI

I first tasted black risotto in Florence, at a small restaurant beside the River Arno. The risotto was served with delicious sautéed scallops, and since then I have had many attempts at making an equally stunning dish at home. This is my favourite risotto, coloured jet black with the ink from the squid, and the squid itself cut into the shape of fine white spaghetti, sautéed lightly with olive oil, lemon and garlic. It makes a sensational picture on a plate

If you are unable to find squid with their ink sacs intact, use 3 × 30 ml/1 fl oz sachets of squid ink, bought separately.

SERVES 4

SQUID SPAGHETTI
350 g/12 oz squid, with ink sacs intact
4 tablespoons extra virgin olive oil
1 clove garlic, crushed
freshly squeezed juice of 1 lemon
2 tablespoons finely chopped parsley
freshly ground black pepper

RISOTTO
2 tablespoons extra virgin olive oil
1 shallot, finely chopped
2 cloves garlic, finely chopped
250 g/8 oz arborio rice
90 ml/3 fl oz dry white wine
900 ml/1½ pints hot fish stock
freshly ground sea salt and black pepper

Clean the squid, removing the ink sacs, tentacles, membrane and quill. Extract the ink from the ink sacs and reserve until later. Pat the squid dry, then cut lengthways down one side and open out. Cut lengthways into fine julienne strips, so that when cooked it will resemble spaghetti.

To make the spaghetti, warm the oil in a large frying pan with the garlic added to flavour the oil. Add the squid spaghetti and briefly sauté over a moderate heat for about 1½ minutes, without allowing it to colour. Remove from the heat and add the lemon juice and chopped parsley. Season to taste with black pepper.

To make the risotto, warm the oil in a large, heavy-based saucepan, then add the shallot and garlic. Sweat over a low heat until soft and translucent, but not coloured. Stir in the arborio rice and cook for 2–3 minutes, until translucent.

Add the white wine and stir well until all the wine has been absorbed by the rice. Begin adding the fish stock over a moderate heat, one ladleful at a time and stirring well after each addition, until all the stock has been absorbed by the rice. Carry on adding more stock as each ladleful is absorbed. Stir the squid ink into the risotto with the last ladleful of stock. After about 15-20 minutes the rice should be tender, but still al dente, with all the stock and the ink absorbed. Season to taste with salt and pepper.

Serve the black risotto in deep bowls, with the white squid spaghetti on top, and the lemon and parsley juices drizzled over the risotto.

TAGLIATELLE TRICOLORE

THREE-COLOURED TAGLIATELLE

This colourful pasta dish is oozing with the vibrant Italian flavours of sun-dried tomatoes, toasted pine nuts, baby spinach and radicchio. It look and tastes absolutely wonderful. Spinach and radicchio are extremely rich sources of vitamins C and beta-carotene, while black olives and pine nuts contain high levels of vitamin E.

SERVES 4

6 sun-dried tomatoes in olive oil, roughly chopped
90 g/3 oz pine nuts
100 ml/3½ fl oz extra virgin olive oil
2 shallots, finely chopped
2 cloves garlic, crushed
125 g/4 oz baby spinach leaves, stalks removed and cut into long, thin strips
125 g/4 oz radicchio, cut into long, thin strips
sea salt
150 g/5 oz pink tagliatelle
150 g/5 oz green tagliatelle
150 g/5 oz white tagliatelle
125 g/4 oz black olives
2 tablespoons finely chopped flat-leaf parsley
60 g/2 oz freshly grated Parmesan cheese

Place the sun-dried tomatoes in a food processor or blender and process until reduced to a thick purée.

Place the pine nuts in a dry saucepan and toast lightly over a moderate heat until golden.

Warm 2 tablespoons of olive oil in a large saucepan, then add the shallots and garlic. Sweat over a low heat for 4–5 minutes, until soft and translucent, but not coloured. Add the sun-dried tomatoes and pine nuts, mixing well. Add the spinach and radicchio strips. Cook for 1 minute, then cover and leave to wilt for about 5 minutes.

Bring a large saucepan of lightly salted water to the boil, then stir in the 3 kinds of tagliatelle. Cook the pasta over fairly high heat for 7–8 minutes until it is al dente.

Add the remaining olive oil to the saucepan containing the spinach and radicchio mixture, then add the black olives and parsley and warm through for about 1 minute.

Drain the tagliatelle and place in a large, warm bowl, then pour over the sauce, tossing well. Serve in individual bowls, sprinkled with freshly grated Parmesan.

PAELLA A LA VALENCIANA

CLASSIC VALENCIAN PAELLA

Valencian paella was originally a humble peasant dish cooked on an open fire of burning wood, deriving its name from the large two-handed pan, called a *paellera*, in which the rice is cooked. Today, paella has developed into a dish of international renown and in Spain it is traditionally served at family celebrations or social gatherings, where huge paelleras are served brimming with saffron-scented rice and a delicious medley of seafood and chicken, accompanied by sangria or red wine.

SERVES 6–8

1.75 kg/3½ lb free-range chicken, jointed into 16 small pieces
200 ml/7 fl oz extra virgin olive oil
12 large raw prawns in their shells
1 large onion, finely chopped
5 cloves garlic, finely chopped
3 red peppers, cored, seeded and cut lengthways into strips
750 g/1½ lb tomatoes, skinned, seeded and coarsely chopped
2 squid, cleaned and cut into rings, tentacles chopped
500 g/1 lb Valencia rice or arborio rice
1.3 litres/2¼ pints hot chicken stock
2 pinches of saffron threads
1 teaspoon paprika
125 g/4 oz shelled fresh peas
freshly ground sea salt and black pepper
12 mussels in their shells, scrubbed and beards removed
12 clams in their shells, scrubbed
2 lemons, cut into wedges

Pat the chicken dry on kitchen paper and season lightly. Warm half the olive oil in a paellera or very large frying pan, then add the chicken pieces. Sauté over a moderate heat for 8–10 minutes, until golden brown all over. Remove the chicken from the pan with a slotted spoon and keep warm. Add the prawns to the paellera and sauté until they turn pink, then remove with a slotted spoon and keep warm.

Pour the remaining olive oil into the paellera, then add the onion, garlic, red peppers and tomatoes. Add the squid rings and the tentacles to the pan. Sauté with the vegetables over a moderate heat for 4–5 minutes.

Add the rice, stirring well for 1½–2 minutes, then pour in the hot stock, saffron threads, paprika and peas, seasoning with salt and pepper. Return the chicken pieces to the pan, then cover and simmer over a moderate heat for 10 minutes, without stirring.

After 10 minutes, add the mussels, clams and prawns, pressing them down into the rice, without stirring. Cover and cook for a further 10 minutes, until all the liquid has been absorbed and the rice is plump and dry. Discard any mussels and clams that have failed to open. Remove the pan from the heat, then cover with a clean dry tea towel and leave to settle for 8–10 minutes. Place some lemon wedges over the rice and serve straight from the paellera.

TRENETTE AL PESTO

TRENETTE WITH BASIL, PINE NUTS, GARLIC AND OLIVE OIL

Although this wonderful basil sauce so adored by the Genoese is renowned world-wide, let us not forget that its origins are humble and it should traditionally be made by hand with a pestle and mortar. If you are really pushed for time, you can of course use a food processor, but I still feel that the hand-made version brings out the flavours best.

SERVES 4

90 g/3 oz basil leaves, coarsely torn
3 cloves garlic, coarsely chopped
45 g/1½ oz pine nuts
4 twists of freshly ground sea salt
90 g/3 oz freshly grated Parmesan cheese
150 ml/¼ pint extra virgin olive oil
500 g/1 lb trenette

Place the basil leaves, garlic and pine nuts in a mortar. Add the sea salt, then pound well together. When reduced to a pulp, add the Parmesan and continue to pound until smooth. Now slowly add the olive oil in a thin stream, pounding continuously, until blended to a smooth green sauce.

Bring a large saucepan of lightly salted water to the boil, then add the trenette. Cook the pasta over fairly high heat for 7-8 minutes, or until it is al dente. Drain thoroughly, then add the pesto to the trenette and toss well. Serve at once.

PILAFI

GREEK PILAF WITH PINE NUTS AND SULTANAS

This exotic Greek pilaf, scented with bay leaves, combines
the intense flavours of fresh ginger and lemon zest with
sweet sultanas and pine nuts.

SERVES 4

3 tablespoons extra virgin olive oil
2 large onions, finely chopped
4 cloves garlic, finely chopped
2 bay leaves
$^{1}/_{2}$ tablespoon finely chopped fresh root ginger
350 g / 12 oz long-grain rice
900 ml / 1$^{1}/_{2}$ pints hot chicken stock
125 g / 4 oz pine nuts
125 g / 4 oz sultanas
finely grated zest of 1 lemon

Warm the olive oil in a large, heavy-based saucepan, then
add the onions and garlic. Sweat over a low heat for about 5
minutes, until soft and translucent, but not coloured. Add
the bay leaves, ginger and rice and cook for a further 2
minutes, stirring well.

Pour the hot chicken stock on to the rice, bring to the
boil, then cover and simmer over a moderate heat for about
15 minutes, without stirring, until all the liquid has been
absorbed and the rice is plump and dry.

Remove from the heat and stir the pine nuts, sultanas and
lemon zest into the rice. Cover with a clean dry tea towel
and leave to rest for about 10 minutes before serving.

SPAGHETTI CON FRUTTI DI MARE

SPAGHETTI WITH SEAFOOD

This succulent seafood and pasta dish is extremely popular on the Mediterranean shores of Italy, where such a wealth of magnificent fish and shellfish is enjoyed. Add as much of your favourite seafood as you wish – local Italians would add oysters, octopus, langoustines and all sorts of seafood treasures to make their own marvellous concoctions.
Seafood not only has a low saturated fat content, but also provides valuable amounts of protein, B vitamins and the minerals iron, iodine, zinc and selenium.

SERVES 4

24 mussels in their shells, scrubbed and beards removed
24 clams in their shells, scrubbed
425 g/14 oz spaghetti
100 ml/3¹/₂ fl oz extra virgin olive oil
2 cloves garlic, finely chopped
2 squid, cleaned, and cut into rings
175 g/6 oz large raw prawns
2 tablespoons dry white wine
freshly ground sea salt and black pepper
3 tablespoons finely chopped parsley

Discard any shells that are not tightly closed. Place the mussels and clams in a large saucepan, adding just enough water to cover the bottom of the pan. Cover and steam over a fairly high heat for about 5 minutes, until all the shells have opened. Drain the mussels and clams, discarding any that have failed to open, then boil the cooking juices over a fairly high heat until reduced to 1 tablespoon.

Bring a large saucepan of lightly salted water to the boil, then stir in the spaghetti. Cook the pasta over a fairly high heat for 7–8 minutes, or until it is al dente.

Meanwhile, pour the olive oil into a large saucepan and add the chopped garlic. Warm over a low heat for 1-2 minutes, to flavour the oil, without browning the garlic. Add the squid and prawns and sauté gently for about 2 minutes. Add the dry white wine and reduced mussel juices, then season with salt and pepper. Add the mussels and clams, still in their shells, to the saucepan. Cook over a moderate heat for about 1½ minutes.

Drain the spaghetti, then add to the saucepan and toss well with the seafood, mixing well. Serve in deep bowls, sprinkled generously with parsley.

SPAGHETTINI AL ZAFFERANO CON CAPESANTE

SAFFRON SPAGHETTINI WITH SCALLOPS, TOMATOES AND BASIL

Scallops are here served in their shells, on a golden bed of saffron-scented spaghettini, flavoured with tomatoes, basil and olive oil.

SERVES 4

16 scallops with corals in their shells
freshly ground sea salt and black pepper
150 ml/¹/₄ pint extra virgin olive oil
1 clove garlic, crushed
1 teaspoon finely chopped red chilli pepper, seeded
4 tomatoes, skinned, seeded and diced
2 generous handfuls of basil leaves
250 g/8 oz spaghettini
¹/₄ teaspoon saffron threads

Using a knife with a rigid blade, prise open the scallop shells by inserting the blade between the upper and lower shells. Debeard the scallops, then rinse under cold water, leaving the corals intact. Pat dry on kitchen paper, then season lightly with salt and pepper. Scrub 16 of the scallop shells, and reserve for serving.

Place all but 3 tablespoons of the olive oil in a small saucepan, then add the garlic and chilli and warm over a very gentle heat to allow the flavours to infuse. Remove from the heat and add the tomato. Reserve 4 sprigs of basil for garnish, then cut the remainder into fine strips and add to the oil.

Bring a saucepan of lightly salted water to the boil, then stir in the spaghettini and saffron. Cook the pasta over fairly high heat for 7–8 minutes, or until it is al dente.

Warm the remaining olive oil in a large frying pan and sear the scallops over a high heat for just 1 minute on each side, so that they remain succulent and moist.

Warm the scallop shells under a moderate grill, then arrange on individual plates. Drain the spaghettini and place in a large bowl. Pour over the tomato and basil oil, tossing well. Spoon the spaghettini into the scallop shells, then arrange the seared scallops on top. Garnish with the reserved sprigs of basil.

ARROZ CON POLLO

CHICKEN WITH SAFFRON-SCENTED RICE

A speciality of Valencia, home of Spain's most renowned rice dishes, this recipe is immensely popular not only on the Mediterranean coast, but in the rest of Spain and in South American countries too. It is a satisfying, heart-warming dish, easy to prepare and bursting with lovely Mediterranean flavours.

The high levels of complex carbohydrates provided by the rice make a healthy partner for the low-fat protein provided by the chicken.

SERVES 4

1.5 kg/3 lb free-range chicken, jointed into 8 pieces
freshly ground sea salt and black pepper
4 tablespoons extra virgin olive oil
2 large onions, finely chopped
4 cloves garlic, finely chopped
2 large red and 1 large green peppers, cored, seeded and cut lengthways into strips
350 g/12 oz tomatoes, skinned, seeded and coarsely chopped
425 g/14 oz Valencia rice or arborio rice
1 litre/1¾ pints hot chicken stock
¼ teaspoon saffron threads
1 teaspoon paprika
3 tablespoons finely chopped parsley

Pat the chicken pieces dry, then season lightly with salt and pepper. Warm the olive oil in a very large frying pan, or ideally in a paellera, then sauté the chicken pieces over a moderate heat, turning several times, until golden brown all over. Remove the chicken with a slotted spoon and keep warm.

Add the onions, garlic and peppers to the pan and sauté over a moderate heat until soft. Add the tomatoes and continue to cook for a further 4-5 minutes, then stir the rice into the vegetables. Pour in the hot chicken stock with the saffron and paprika, then return the chicken pieces to the pan. Bring to the boil, then cover and simmer over a moderate heat for 20-25 minutes, until the chicken is tender and the rice plump and dry, having absorbed all the liquid.

Remove from the heat, then cover with a clean dry tea towel and leave to rest for about 10 minutes. Sprinkle with fresh parsley just before serving.

FETTUCCINE NERO ALLA ROMANA

BLACK FETTUCCINE WITH RED AND YELLOW PEPPERS AND SEARED SCALLOPS

This lively pasta dish is perfect for an after-work supper party with friends – the enticing fettuccine, coloured black with squid ink, is served with vibrantly coloured, char-grilled red and yellow peppers, and dressed with beautifully moist and succulent quick-seared scallops.

SERVES 4

3 large red peppers, halved, cored and seeded
3 large yellow peppers, halved, cored and seeded
500 g / 1 lb black fettuccine, coloured with squid ink
125 ml / 4 fl oz extra virgin olive oil
1 medium onion, finely chopped
3 cloves garlic, crushed
½ chilli pepper, seeded and finely chopped
freshly ground sea salt and black pepper

SEARED SCALLOPS
12 scallops, shelled
1–2 tablespoons extra virgin olive oil
sprigs of chervil

Place the peppers skin-side up under a hot grill, until the skins have blackened and blistered. Place in a plastic bag and seal. Allow to cool, then peel off the skin and cut lengthways into strips, approximately the same width as the fettuccine.

Bring a large saucepan of lightly salted boiling water to the boil, and stir in the black fettuccine. Cook the pasta over a fairly high heat for 7-8 minutes, until it is al dente. (If using fresh pasta, this will only take about 4 minutes).

Gently warm half the olive oil in a large saucepan, then

add the onion, garlic and chilli pepper. Sweat over a low heat for about 5 minutes, until soft but not coloured. Pour in the remaining olive oil and the grilled peppers and keep warm over a very gentle heat.

To make the seared scallops, pat the scallops dry on kitchen paper, then season lightly with salt and pepper. Brush a large frying pan with a small amount of oil, letting the pan get really hot over a high heat, then sear the scallops for less than 1 minute on each side, so that they are golden brown on the outside, but still moist and succulent inside.

Drain the pasta, then add to the peppers in the saucepan, tossing well. Serve the black pasta and peppers on warm plates, with the seared scallops. Garnish with sprigs of fresh chervil.

SPAGHETTI CON FORMAGGIO CAPRINO E POMODORE

SPAGHETTI WITH GOAT'S CHEESE, BASIL AND TOMATOES

Two flavours of tomato, fresh and sun-dried, combined with goat's cheese, basil and garlic, create an exceptionally tasty pasta dish.

SERVES 6

500 g / 1 lb spaghetti
100 ml / 3½ fl oz extra virgin olive oil
3 cloves garlic, finely chopped
1 kg / 2 lb plum tomatoes, skinned, seeded and coarsely chopped
freshly ground sea salt and black pepper
90 g / 3 oz sun-dried tomatoes, drained and chopped
250 g / 8 oz goat's cheese, cut into cubes
2 generous handfuls of basil leaves, coarsely torn

Bring a large saucepan of lightly salted water to the boil, then stir in the spaghetti. Cook the pasta over a fairly high heat for 7–8 minutes, until it is al dente.

While the pasta is cooking, warm the olive oil in a large frying pan, add the garlic and sauté over a low heat for 1-2 minutes, until soft but not coloured. Add the chopped tomatoes, season with salt and pepper, and cook over a moderate heat for about 5 minutes, until reduced to a thick pulp. Stir in the sun-dried tomatoes.

Drain the pasta and transfer to a large bowl. Pour over the tomato and garlic sauce and toss well. Stir in the goat's cheese and basil leaves and serve at once.

TAGLIATELLE ALLA MARINARA

FISHERMAN'S TAGLIATELLE WITH MUSSELS AND GARLIC

This simple pasta dish is laden with the classic flavours of mussels, garlic and parsley that have grown to symbolize traditional Mediterranean 'fisherman-style' cuisine.

SERVES

1 kg/2 lb mussels in their shells, scrubbed and beards removed
425 g/14 oz tagliatelle
150 ml/¼ pint extra virgin olive oil
3 cloves garlic, crushed
4 tablespoons finely chopped parsley
freshly ground sea salt and black pepper

Discard any mussel shells that are not tightly closed. Put the mussels in a large saucepan, adding just enough water to cover the bottom of the pan. Cover and steam over a fairly high heat for about 5 minutes, until all the shells have opened. Drain the mussels and reserve the cooking juices. Shell the mussels, reserving 8 unshelled mussels for garnish. Discard any that have failed to open.

Bring a large saucepan of lightly salted water to the boil, then stir in the tagliatelle. Cook the pasta over fairly high heat for 7–8 minutes, until it is al dente.

Meanwhile, warm the olive oil in a large saucepan and add the garlic. Swirl the garlic around in the oil for 2–3 minutes over a low heat, to allow the garlic to flavour the oil.

Drain the tagliatelle and return to a clean saucepan. Pour over the garlic-scented oil, along with the mussels and 2 tablespoons of their reserved juices, the fresh parsley and black pepper. Toss well and heat for 1-2 minutes, to warm through. Serve in bowls, garnished with the reserved mussels.

FETTUCCINE ALLE ERBE

FETTUCCINE WITH HERBS

The pure simplicity of this pasta dish, redolent with the wonderful flavours of fresh herbs, makes it very appealing.

SERVES 4

500 g / 1 lb fettuccine
60 g / 2 oz freshly grated Pecorino cheese

HERB SAUCE
generous handful of basil leaves
generous handful of flat-leaf parsley
6 mint leaves
3 cloves garlic, crushed
2 tablespoons capers, drained
6 anchovy fillets in olive oil, drained
1 teaspoon Dijon mustard
175 ml / 6 fl oz extra virgin olive oil
2 tablespoons balsamic vinegar
freshly ground sea salt and black pepper

To make the herb sauce, place the basil, parsley and mint leaves in a food processor or blender and process until coarsely chopped. Add the garlic, capers, anchovies and Dijon mustard and process again until smooth. With the motor still running, slowly add the olive oil in a thin stream until a smooth, homogenous consistency is obtained, then add the balsamic vinegar. Season generously with black pepper.

Bring a large saucepan of lightly salted water to the boil, then stir in the fettuccine. Cook the pasta over a fairly high heat for 7–8 minutes, until it is al dente. Drain the pasta and transfer to a large, warm bowl. Pour over the herb sauce and toss well. Sprinkle the Pecorino cheese on top and serve immediately.

7
Vegetables

PEPERONATA

BRAISED RED AND YELLOW PEPPERS

This makes a really well-flavoured vegetarian dish, with the peppers served either on their own with chunks of whole-meal country bread, or with pasta. Peperonata also makes a delicious accompaniment to grilled chicken. I think the flavours are best when the peppers are served lukewarm rather than cold.

SERVES 4

175 ml/6 fl oz extra virgin olive oil
1 large onion, finely chopped
2 cloves garlic, finely chopped
4 large red peppers, cored, seeded and cut lengthways into strips
3 large yellow peppers, cored, seeded and cut lengthways into strips
500 g/1 lb plum tomatoes, skinned, seeded and coarsely chopped
freshly ground sea salt and black pepper
2 tablespoons capers, drained
generous handful of basil leaves, coarsely torn

Warm 125 ml/4 fl oz of the olive oil in a large, heavy-based saucepan, then add the onion and garlic. Sweat over a low heat until soft and translucent, but not coloured.

Add the peppers to the pan and cook over a moderate heat for about 15 minutes, until the peppers are tender. Add the tomatoes and cook for a further 15 minutes, stirring from time to time. Season with salt and pepper.

Remove from the heat and allow to cool until lukewarm, then stir the remaining olive oil, the capers and the basil into the braised peppers. Serve at room temperature, or alternatively serve cold.

PUREE DE POMMES DE TERRE A L'AIL

MASHED POTATOES WITH GARLIC AND OLIVE OIL

A healthy alternative to traditional mashed potatoes, laden with cream and butter but unfortunately high in saturated fat, is something I have always longed for. For me, this delectably creamy dish of potatoes flavoured with garlic and puréed with fromage frais and olive oil, is the perfect choice.

SERVES 4–6

1 kg/2 lb potatoes (the variety Maris Piper is excellent for mashed potatoes, giving a lovely smooth texture)
6 cloves garlic
1 tablespoon fromage frais
150 ml/¹/₄ pint extra virgin olive oil
freshly ground sea salt and black pepper
2 tablespoons finely chopped parsley

Cook the potatoes and garlic together in a large saucepan of lightly salted boiling water, until soft. Drain, then mash the potatoes, garlic and fromage frais together until smooth. Add the olive oil, then using a large balloon whisk, purée the potatoes until smooth. If necessary, add more olive oil to give the potatoes a light, creamy consistency. Season generously with black pepper and more salt, if necessary. Sprinkle with chopped parsley just before serving.

ESPINACAS A LA CATALANA

WILTED SPINACH, CATALAN-STYLE

Pine nuts are often used in Catalan food. Lightly toasted, they make a lovely addition to this dish of spinach wilted in its own juices, then tossed in warm olive oil and a squeeze of lemon. Wilting the spinach briefly with no added liquid ensures that it retains the maximum amount of nutrients.

SERVES 4

1 kg/2 lb spinach, tough stems removed
freshly ground sea salt and black pepper
3 tablespoons pine nuts
3 tablespoons extra virgin olive oil
freshly squeezed juice of ¹/₂ lemon

Rinse the spinach under cold running water, then place in a large saucepan. Season with salt and pepper, then cover and leave to wilt over a moderate heat for about 3 minutes.

Lightly toast the pine nuts under a medium hot grill.

Warm the olive oil in a small saucepan set over a low heat, then add the toasted pine nuts. Pour the oil and pine nuts over the spinach and toss well. Squeeze the lemon juice over the spinach and serve at once.

OIGNONS ROUGES GRILLES AU ROSMARIN

GRILLED RED ONIONS WITH ROSEMARY

Balsamic vinegar and a hint of rosemary make great flavour enhancers for red onions. With their deeply pigmented skin, red onions have exceptionally strong antioxidant properties.

SERVES 4–6

125 ml/4 fl oz extra virgin olive oil
2 tablespoons rosemary leaves
1 kg/2 lb red onions, cut crossways into 1 cm/½ inch slices
4 tablespoons balsamic vinegar
freshly ground sea salt and black pepper
2 tablespoons finely chopped parsley

Place the olive oil and rosemary in a small saucepan and warm very gently over a low heat, then remove from the heat and allow the flavours to infuse for about 10 minutes. Strain the oil.

Brush the onions lightly all over with half the rosemary-scented oil, then grill under a moderately high heat for about 3–4 minutes on each side, until tender and just lightly charred.

Whisk the remaining oil with the balsamic vinegar, seasoning lightly. Arrange the grilled red onions on a serving dish, then drizzle over the balsamic and rosemary dressing. Sprinkle with chopped fresh parsley and serve lukewarm.

FINOCCHIO BRASATO

BRAISED FENNEL

Fennel is an extremely popular vegetable in both Italy and France. It has a gorgeous flavour, strong and aromatic, that responds well to different cooking methods. Always use the green feathery tops from the fennel to sprinkle over the vegetable when cooked.

SERVES 4

4 tablespoons extra virgin olive oil
4 fennel bulbs, quartered, with feathery leaves reserved
150 ml / ¼ pint vegetable stock
freshly ground sea salt and black pepper

Warm the olive oil in a large saucepan, add the fennel, cover and sweat over a low heat for about 15 minutes.

Pour in the vegetable stock, season with salt and pepper and braise for a further 15 minutes or so, until the fennel is soft and almost all the liquid has been absorbed.

Finely chop the reserved fennel leaves and sprinkle over just before serving.

FINOCCHIO AL FORNO

ROASTED FENNEL

A valuable source of potassium, fennel has natural diuretic properties and can help to alleviate water retention problems and improve digestion as well. It is also a good source of antioxidant vitamin beta-carotene, folic acid and fibre.

SERVES 4

4 fennel bulbs, sliced in 4 lengthways, feathery leaves reserved
4 tablespoons extra virgin olive oil
freshly ground sea salt and black pepper

Preheat the oven to 180°C/350°F/Gas Mark 4.

Brush the fennel generously all over with the olive oil. Lay the fennel in an ovenproof dish, season lightly, then pour over the remaining olive oil. Roast in the preheated oven for 15–20 minutes, until tender.

Finely chop the reserved feathery leaves and sprinkle over just before serving.

FINOCCHIO ALLA GRIGLIA

GRILLED FENNEL

SERVES 4

*4 fennel bulbs, sliced lengthways in 4, feathery leaves reserved
extra virgin olive oil*

Brush the fennel generously with olive oil, then place under
a medium hot grill until lightly charred and tender. Drizzle
lightly with olive oil and sprinkle with the feathery leaves,
finely chopped.

JUDIAS SALTEADAS

GREEN BEANS TOSSED IN OLIVE OIL AND GARLIC

'Jumping green beans', lightly steamed and enriched with garlic-scented olive oil, make a great accompaniment to grilled chicken and fish.

Green beans are an excellent source of the B vitamins, anti-oxidant vitamin C and the minerals potassium and zinc, providing a healthy dose of fibre as well. Steaming the beans ensures that the vitamin content is preserved.

SERVES 4–6

500 g / 1 lb green beans
125 ml / 4 fl oz extra virgin olive oil
3 cloves garlic, crushed
1 small onion, finely chopped
freshly ground sea salt and black pepper
1 tablespoon finely chopped mint leaves

Steam the green beans over fiercely boiling water for several minutes, until tender, but still crisp and al dente.

Gently warm the olive oil in a large saucepan, then add the garlic and onion. Sweat over a very low heat, until soft and translucent, but not coloured. Add the steamed green beans to the pan and toss well. Season with salt and pepper, then add the chopped mint and serve at once.

FUNGHI AL FORNO ALLA PARMIGIANA

OVEN-BAKED MUSHROOMS WITH PARMESAN AND HERBS

Italy is home to some of the finest mushroom dishes. Usually they are quite simple, requiring little preparation, but the combined flavours always reach the height of perfection.

SERVES 4

500 g / 1 lb mixed wild mushrooms, large ones halved
2 tablespoons freshly grated Parmesan cheese
1 tablespoon breadcrumbs, made from day-old bread
¹/₂ tablespoon chopped rosemary
¹/₂ tablespoon chopped thyme
1 tablespoon chopped flat-leaf parsley
1 clove garlic, finely chopped
freshly ground sea salt and black pepper
2–3 tablespoons extra virgin olive oil

Preheat the oven to 180°C/350°F/Gas Mark 4.

Arrange the mushrooms in a lightly oiled ovenproof baking dish. Mix together the Parmesan, breadcrumbs, herbs and garlic, seasoning lightly with salt and pepper. Spoon the mixture over the mushrooms, then drizzle generously all over with olive oil. Place the dish in the preheated oven for 10–12 minutes, until the mushrooms are tender and the cheese mixture has formed a golden crust. Serve very hot.

PUREE D'AIL AU FOUR

ROAST GARLIC PURÉE

Puréed garlic enriched with olive oil and parsley makes a delicious accompaniment to roast chicken.

The low incidence of coronary heart disease in Mediterranean countries is partially attributed to the high consumption of garlic.

SERVES 6

3 large heads of garlic
extra virgin olive oil
3 tablespoons finely chopped fresh parsley
freshly ground black pepper

Preheat the oven to 180°/350°/Gas Mark 4.

Wrap each head of garlic individually in foil, then place in the preheated oven and roast for about 25 minutes.

Allow to cool slightly, then remove the foil and break up the garlic into cloves. Peel the skin off, then mash the garlic with a fork to a smooth purée. Add a little olive oil to make the purée more fluid, then season generously with parsley and black pepper.

RATATOUILLE

STEWED PROVENÇAL VEGETABLES

This wonderful symphony of vegetables flavoured with
fresh herbs is delicious served either warm or cold.
The vegetables full of essential vitamins and minerals, notably vitamins C and beta-carotene and the minerals
potassium and folate. The fat content is pure monounsaturated, which unlike saturated fat is actually good for
the heart and circulation.

SERVES 6

750 g/1½ lb aubergines, quartered lengthways, then cut into
1 cm/½ inch slices
freshly ground sea salt and black pepper
150 ml/¼ pint extra virgin olive oil, plus extra to taste
2 large onions, sliced
500 g/1 lb courgettes, sliced into 1 cm/½ inch rounds
3 large red peppers, cored, seeded and sliced lengthways into strips
5 cloves garlic, finely chopped
1 kg/2 lb plum tomatoes, skinned, seeded and coarsely chopped
2 generous handfuls of basil leaves, coarsely torn
1 tablespoon finely chopped parsley
2 sprigs of fresh thyme
1 bay leaf

Sprinkle the aubergines with salt, then place in a colander
and leave for about 30 minutes, to allow the bitter juices to
drain away. Rinse well, then pat dry on kitchen paper.

Warm 3 tablespoons of olive oil in a large saucepan, then
sweat the onions over a low heat for about 5 minutes, until
soft and translucent, but not coloured. Pour in the remaining olive oil, then add the courgettes, red peppers, garlic and
aubergines, and cook over a moderate heat for a further 5

minutes. Add the tomatoes, half the basil, the parsley, thyme, bay leaf and seasoning. Cover and simmer over a low heat for about 20 minutes, stirring from time to time, until the vegetables are tender and the tomatoes have reduced to a thick pulp.

Remove the bay leaf and thyme and allow to cool until lukewarm, then stir in the remaining basil, and more olive oil if liked. Serve warm or cold.

POIREAUX A LA VINAIGRETTE

STEAMED LEEKS WITH LEMON VINAIGRETTE

Leeks are rich in potassium, a mineral that plays a key role in the proper maintenance of healthy cells and nervous tissue. Use as much of the green part of the leek as you can, because the green leafy part has a higher concentration of vitamins and minerals than the white part.

SERVES 4

8 slim leeks
100 ml/3½ fl oz extra virgin olive oil
2 tablespoons freshly squeezed lemon juice
freshly ground sea salt and black pepper

Steam the leeks over lightly salted boiling water for about 8–10 minutes, until just tender.

Whisk the olive oil and lemon juice together until thoroughly emulsified, then season with salt and pepper.

Arrange the leeks in a large serving dish, then pour over the lemon vinaigrette, turning to make sure that they are fully coated. Serve at room temperature.

POMODORO AL FORNO

BAKED TOMATOES

The Italians are masters with tomatoes, enhancing their sweet taste with a simple breadcrumb topping flavoured with garlic, parsley and olive oil.

SERVES 4

100 ml/3½ fl oz extra virgin olive oil
4 large Mediterranean tomatoes, sliced in half
freshly ground sea salt and black pepper
60 g/2 oz breadcrumbs made from 1-day-old Olive Oil Bread
(see page 244)
3 cloves garlic, crushed
4 tablespoons finely chopped fresh parsley

Preheat the oven to 190°/375°/Gas Mark 5.

Warm half the olive oil in a large frying pan, then place the tomatoes, cut-side down, in the oil, and sauté over a gentle heat for about 4 minutes. Remove the tomatoes from the saucepan and place in an ovenproof baking dish, seasoning lightly with salt and pepper.

Mix together the breadcrumbs, garlic and parsley, then spoon over the tomatoes. Drizzle the remaining olive oil on top, then bake in the preheated oven for about 10 minutes, until the tomatoes are tender but still retain their shape. Remove from the oven and serve at once.

BROCOLIS AUX AMANDES

BROCCOLI WITH ALMONDS

A vegetable dish of broccoli with almonds is a classic favourite in France. This more modern recipe serves the
broccoli and almonds with a tomato and garlic vinaigrette,
which I think adds the perfect finishing touch.
Broccoli is one of the cruciferous family of vegetables, rich
in chemical compounds believed to block the formation of
nitrosamines, destructive carcinogens capable of causing
extensive damage to body cells and tissues.

SERVES 4

750 g/1½ lb broccoli, divided into florets
60 g/2 oz flaked almonds, lightly toasted

TOMATO VINAIGRETTE
4 plum tomatoes, skinned and seeded
125 ml/4 fl oz extra virgin olive oil
1 tablespoon freshly squeezed lemon juice
1 clove garlic, crushed
freshly ground sea salt and black pepper

To make the vinaigrette, press 2 plum tomatoes through
a nylon sieve to extract the juice. Whisk the olive oil and
lemon juice together until thoroughly emulsified, then stir
in the tomato juice and the garlic. Finely dice the remaining
tomatoes, then add to the vinaigrette. Season to taste with
salt and pepper.

Steam the broccoli over lightly salted boiling water for
about 3 minutes, until just tender, but still firm and al dente.
Place the broccoli in a warm serving dish and drizzle
the tomato vinaigrette on top. Sprinkle with the toasted
almonds and serve at once.

PATATAS BRAVAS

FIERY POTATOES

Not for the faint-hearted, this hot potato dish was created centuries ago by the gypsies in Moorish Andalucia, who skilfully mastered the technique of making inexpensive foods taste really special. Modern times have made this into a popular tapas dish in Spanish bars.

The skins are left on the potatoes to obtain maximum nutrients, as the highest concentration of vitamins and minerals is stored under the skin.

SERVES 4

750 g / 1½ lb waxy potatoes, cut into bite-sized pieces
125 ml / 4 fl oz extra virgin olive oil

FIERY SAUCE
2 tablespoons tomato purée
2 tablespoons red wine vinegar
2 tablespoons extra virgin olive oil
2 teaspoons sweet paprika
a pinch or more of cayenne pepper, according to taste

Pat the potatoes dry with kitchen paper, to absorb any moisture.

Warm the olive oil in a large frying pan, then add the potato pieces. Sauté over a moderate heat, turning from time to time, until crisp and golden. When the potatoes are cooked, remove from the heat and pour off any oil remaining in the frying pan.

Mix all the sauce ingredients together, then pour into the frying pan. Return to the heat and cook for about 2 minutes, until the sauce has reduced to a thick red consistency. Stir well so that the potatoes are thoroughly coated with the hot sauce. Serve warm.

ECHALOTES AU VINAIGRE D'XERES

CARAMELIZED SHALLOTS WITH SHERRY-SCENTED VINEGAR

With their sweet and sour flavour, these caramelized shallots make a good accompaniment to grilled chicken.
Like all members of the onion family, shallots are recognized as having many health-giving properties. Containing strong antioxidant and anti-bacterial nutrients, shallots can help to build up the immune system, reduce the level of cholesterol in the blood and fight colds and infection.

SERVES 4–6

3 tablespoons extra virgin olive oil
500 g / 1 lb shallots, left whole
4 tablespoons sherry vinegar
200 ml / 7 fl oz water
2 cloves
1 bay leaf
1 tablespoon brown sugar

Warm the olive oil in a large saucepan, then add the shallots. Gently sauté over a moderate heat until just beginning to colour. Add the sherry vinegar, water, cloves, bay leaf and sugar to the pan. Simmer over a moderate heat for about 20 minutes until nearly all the liquid has been absorbed and has reduced to a light syrupy consistency. Serve hot.

8
Desserts

BANANES EN PAPILLOTE

BAKED BANANAS EN PAPILLOTE

Baked bananas in sealed parcels are simple to make yet so delicious – the wonderful aroma of the fruit, vanilla and cinnamon only escaping when the parcels are opened.
Bananas are a rich source of potassium, an important mineral required by the body for normal nerve and muscle function.

SERVES 4

4 bananas
4 dessertspoons demerara sugar
2 oranges, peel and pith removed, and cut into segments
3 tablespoons freshly squeezed orange juice
1 tablespoon freshly squeezed lemon juice
1 vanilla pod, split lengthways and cut into 4 pieces
2 cinnamon sticks, each cut into 4 pieces
fromage frais, to serve

Cut out 4 large circles of greaseproof paper, about 30cm/ 12 inches in diameter, and oil lightly. Preheat the oven to 180°C/350°F/Gas Mark 4.

Halve the bananas lengthways and place each banana on one of the paper circles. Sprinkle the bananas with a little demerara sugar, then arrange the orange segments alongside the bananas. Mix the orange juice and lemon juice, then drizzle over the fruit, to moisten it lightly. Lay a piece of vanilla pod and a piece of cinnamon over the fruit, then bring the edges of the greaseproof paper together, closing tightly to form sealed parcels. Bake in the preheated oven for 8-10 minutes.

Serve the bananas in their sealed parcels, to be opened at the table, and serve a bowl of fromage frais separately.

ZABAGLIONE

WARM MARSALA-FLAVOURED CUSTARD WITH AMARETTI

A classic Italian dessert, soothing, warming and wonderfully intoxicating. Crisp Italian macaroons go perfectly with it. Medical opinion differs on how many eggs it is safe to eat, so the advice must be to reserve this luscious dessert for special occasions only.

SERVES 4

6 egg yolks
4 tablespoons caster sugar
175 ml/6 fl oz Marsala
amaretti, to serve

Place the egg yolks and sugar in a large heat-resistant bowl and whisk well until pale and frothy. Stand the bowl over a saucepan of gently simmering water or in the top of a double boiler and gradually whisk in the Marsala. Continue whisking until the mixture has tripled in volume and has become creamy and fluffy.

Pour into tall, stemmed glasses and serve at once, while still warm. Serve the zabaglione accompanied by a plate of amaretti.

FRAISES AU VIN ROUGE

STRAWBERRIES IN RED WINE

This unlikely combination really is quite superb. Left to macerate in the red wine, the strawberries acquire a rich depth of flavour while the wine becomes more mellow and fruity. Obviously, the better the wine, the better the flavour: a good Beaujolais or Claret make an ideal choice.

SERVES 6

1 kg/2 lb strawberries, hulled
3–4 tablespoons caster sugar
¼ bottle red wine

Cut the strawberries in half, so that their juices are released, then dredge with caster sugar. Place in a bowl, pour over the red wine and leave to macerate for about 30 minutes. Serve in stemmed wine glasses.

Variation:

FRAISES AU CHAMPAGNE

STRAWBERRIES IN CHAMPAGNE

Sprinkle the strawberries with caster sugar and leave to rest for about 30 minutes. Spoon the strawberries into tall champagne flutes, then pour chilled champagne over the fruit at the table, so that your guests can enjoy the pleasure of watching the bubbles cascade over the strawberries in a wonderfully sensuous way.

TARTA DE PINONES

ALMOND AND PINE NUT TART

Both almonds and pine nuts are extremely popular in
Spanish cuisine, and the two nuts combine beautifully in
this delicious sweet tart, perfumed with orange.

SERVES 6

275 g/9 oz shortcrust pastry
175 g/6 oz unblanched almonds
60 g/2 oz sugar
finely grated zest of 1 large orange
2 eggs, separated
2 teaspoons orange flower water
2 tablespoons clear honey
2 tablespoons extra virgin olive oil
125 g/4 oz pine nuts

Preheat the oven to 200°C/400°F/Gas Mark 6.

Roll out the pastry on a lightly floured board and use to
line a 23cm/9 inch loose-bottomed tart tin. Prick the base
all over with a fork, then cover with greaseproof paper and
fill with dried peas or beans. Bake blind for 15 minutes, then
remove and discard the paper and beans. Lower the oven
temperature to 190°C/375°F/Gas Mark 5.

Blanch the almonds, then pat dry and grind very finely,
using a food processor. Add the sugar and orange zest, then
make a well in the centre and add the egg yolks, orange
flower water, honey and olive oil. Mix to make a smooth,
thick batter, then stir in two-thirds of the pine nuts. Whisk
the egg whites until stiff, then fold into the batter.

Pour into the prepared pastry case, then sprinkle the
remaining pine nuts on top. Bake for 25–30 minutes, until
the filling is set and the pastry golden brown. Serve warm.

ANANAS AU KIRSCH

PINEAPPLE IN KIRSCH

All fresh fruits are delicious eaten unsweetened, but often a liqueur can help to bring out and enhance a fruit's own special flavour. Pineapple is no exception, and Kirsch enriches the wonderful flavour of fresh pineapple.
Pineapple contains an important enzyme known as bromelain that helps to break down protein and so aid digestion. The fruit provides useful amounts of vitamin C, as well as small amounts of the minerals manganese and potassium.

SERVES 4

1 large ripe pineapple, chilled
4–6 tablespoons Kirsch

Slice the top and bottom off the pineapple, reserve the tuft of leaves for decoration. Slice off all the skin, using a sharp knife. Cut the pineapple lengthways into quarters and remove the hard central core and any small brown 'eyes' that you may have missed when removing the skin.

Cut evenly into slices and arrange on a large serving platter. Drizzle the Kirsch all over the fruit and decorate the platter with the reserved tuft of leaves.

RIZOGALO

AROMATIC RICE PUDDING

Derived from the resin of the lentisc tree, mastic grains have for centuries been highly prized in Greece and Eastern Mediterranean regions as a flavouring for puddings, particularly rice-based ones. With its exotic, aromatic taste, it adds a mysterious Eastern flavour to this creamy rice pudding.

SERVES 6

90 g / 3 oz short-grain rice
1.5 litres / 2½ pints milk
finely pared zest of 1 large orange
1 vanilla pod, split lengthways
3 tablespoons clear honey
2 grains of mastic
1 tablespoon brown sugar
90 g / 3 oz shelled pistachio nuts, coarsely chopped

Soak the rice in cold water for about 30 minutes, then rinse well and drain.

Place the milk, orange zest, vanilla pod and honey in a large saucepan and heat to boiling point. Add the rice, stir well, then reduce the heat and simmer over a very low heat for about 45 minutes, stirring from time to time, until the rice is soft and creamy and almost all the milk has evaporated.

Pound the grains of mastic and sugar together, using a pestle and mortar, until ground to a fine powder. Remove the orange zest and vanilla pod with a slotted spoon, then stir the ground mastic mixture into the rice. Cover with clingfilm and chill well. Serve sprinkled with pistachio nuts.

DOLCE DI RICOTTA

RICOTTA WITH HONEY AND PINE NUTS

Made in minutes, this simple Italian concoction makes a
delicious standby dessert for unexpected guests.
Ricotta provides valuable amounts of protein and is a rich
source of calcium. Its saturated fat content of around 11 per
cent is relatively low compared to the 35 per cent of hard
cheeses such as Cheddar.

SERVES 4

350 g/12 oz fresh ricotta
finely grated zest of 1 lemon
clear honey
60 g/2 oz pine nuts, lightly toasted

Beat the ricotta lightly until smooth, then mix in the grated
lemon zest. Shape the cheese into small mounds with
the aid of 2 tablespoons then place the cheese mounds on
individual serving plates. Drizzle some clear honey over the
ricotta, then sprinkle with lightly toasted pine nuts.

FICHI AL BAROLO

FIGS POACHED IN RED WINE

A lovely rustic Italian dessert, laden with rich flavours.

SERVES 4

750 ml/1¼ pints red wine
175 g/6 oz granulated sugar
12 fresh figs

Place the red wine and sugar in a large, heavy-based saucepan and bring slowly to the boil, stirring well until all the sugar has dissolved. Reduce the heat to simmering point, then place the figs upright in the wine and simmer for about 8 minutes, until the figs are tender, but not too soft.

Remove the figs from the saucepan with a slotted spoon and place on a large serving platter. Boil the remaining red wine over a moderate heat until reduced to a light syrupy consistency. Pour the reduced wine over the figs and serve lukewarm.

ENSALADA VALENCIANA

VALENCIAN CITRUS FRUIT SALAD

Basking in the Mediterranean sun, the beautiful orange groves of Valencia are a spectacular sight. Citrus fruits make a lovely year-round dessert and in this popular salad, the fruits are left to macerate in a honey and lemon dressing, allowing all the lovely juices to run and the flavours to blend beautifully together.

Prized for centuries as an elixir of youth and good health, honey is believed to have antiseptic, antiviral and decongestant properties, and is a particularly useful remedy for chest complaints.

SERVES 6

8 juicy Valencia oranges, peeled, pith removed and sliced into rounds, juices reserved
2 grapefruit, peeled, pith removed and sliced into rounds, juices reserved
freshly squeezed juice of 2 lemons
finely grated zest of 1 lemon
6 tablespoons clear honey
1 tablespoon orange-flower water
250 g/8 oz strawberries, hulled and halved

Arrange the citrus fruit in a large serving bowl.

Mix the lemon juice, lemon zest, honey and orange-flower water with the reserved orange and grapefruit juices, stirring well. Pour over the fruit and leave to macerate in the refrigerator for at least 1 hour.

Just before serving, add the strawberries to the fruit salad.

PESCHE GRATINATE

GRILLED PEACHES WITH AMARETTO

Peach lovers will adore this luscious Italian dessert. The almond liqueur enriches the flavour of the peaches in a most indulgent way.

Peaches are an excellent source of vitamins and minerals, notable vitamins C and beta-carotene, and the mineral potassium. Grilling the peaches for just a short time ensures that all the valuable nutrients are preserved – canned peaches on the other hand lose up to 80 per cent of their natural vitamin and mineral content.

SERVES 4

6 ripe peaches, halved and stoned
freshly squeezed juice of 2 lemons
2 tablespoons caster sugar
150 ml /¼ pint Amaretto
crème fraîche, to serve

Brush the peaches all over with the juice of one of the lemons, then toss in caster sugar.

Arrange the peaches in a shallow, heat-resistant baking dish, cut side up. Place under a medium grill and grill for about 2 minutes, then turn and grill for a further 2 minutes. Pour the Amaretto over the peaches and grill for a further 2–3 minutes. When done, the skin should be golden brown and the flesh soft and tender.

Arrange the peach halves on warm serving plates. Place the baking dish over a moderate heat and stir in the juice of the remaining lemon. Boil the juices until reduced by half. Drizzle the juices over the peaches and serve warm, accompanied by some crème fraîche.

PERAS AL RIOJA

PEARS POACHED IN RED WINE

In this simple yet elegant dessert, pears are poached in a rich medium of red wine with hints of cinnamon, cloves and lemon, absorbing wonderful depths of flavour and colour. Red wine is generally believed to be good for the heart and drinking 2-3 glasses a day is thought to be beneficial to good health.

SERVES 6

6 firm, evenly sized pears, stems intact
freshly squeezed juice of 1 lemon
750 ml/1¼ pints Rioja or other full-bodied dry red wine
150 g/5 oz granulated sugar
1 stick of cinnamon
3 cloves
pared zest of 1 lemon

Peel and core the pears, leaving them whole with stems intact. Brush the fruit all over with lemon juice.

Place the red wine, sugar, cinnamon stick, cloves and lemon zest in a large saucepan and bring slowly to the boil, stirring constantly until all the sugar has dissolved. Reduce the heat to simmering point, then stand the pears upright in the saucepan and cover. Poach the pears very gently for about 20–25 minutes, until they are tender but not too soft, or in any way disintegrating. Remove the pears with a slotted spoon and place in a large serving bowl.

Boil the red wine cooking juices over a moderate heat until reduced to a light, syrupy consistency. Strain the syrup over the pears and serve thoroughly chilled.

PESCHE RIPIENE

STUFFED PEACHES

One of Italy's most popular desserts – a delicious con-coction of ripe, juicy peaches stuffed with ricotta and crumbled amaretti, glazed under a hot grill with a honey and lemon topping.

SERVES 4

6 amaretti biscuits
60 g/2 oz ricotta
2 tablespoons clear honey
freshly squeezed juice of $\frac{1}{2}$ large lemon
4 large ripe peaches, halved and stoned
sprigs of fresh mint, to decorate

Leave the amaretti biscuits in their wrappers and crush lightly with a rolling pin. Fold the crumbled amaretti into the ricotta.

Mix the honey and lemon juice together, then brush the cut side of the peaches with the mixture. Lay the peaches, cut side up, in a shallow baking dish. Spoon the ricotta and amaretti filling into the peach cavities, then drizzle the remaining honey and lemon over the filling. Place under a medium hot grill for about 5 minutes, until golden brown.

Serve at once, decorated with mint sprigs.

GRATIN DES FRUITS D'ETE

SUMMER FRUIT GRATIN

A gratin of fresh fruits makes a sumptuous dinner party dessert, yet is so simple and quick to make. A selection of beautiful, juicy summer fruits are served nesting on a bed of raspberry purée and glazed with a warm, champagne-scented sabayon.

SERVES 4

2 oranges, peeled, pith removed and cut into segments
175 g/6 oz strawberries, hulled
1 fresh fig, cut into 8 segments
1 ripe mango, peeled, stoned and cut into fine slices
1 banana, peeled and sliced

RASPBERRY PUREE
250 g/8 oz raspberries
freshly squeezed juice of 1 lemon
45 g/1½ oz caster sugar

SABAYON
4 egg yolks
60 g/2 oz caster sugar
150 ml/¼ pint champagne brut

To make the raspberry purée, place the raspberries, lemon juice and sugar in a food processor or blender and process to a smooth purée. Strain through a nylon sieve. Spoon a layer of raspberry purée into 4 individual gratin dishes, then arrange the various fruits on top.

To make the sabayon, place the egg yolks and sugar in a heat-resistant bowl, then place the bowl over a bain-marie of gently simmering water or in the top of a double boiler. Whisk until thick and creamy, then gradually whisk in the champagne. Continue whisking until the sabayon thickens and becomes creamy and fluffy (this will take about 10-12 minutes).

Pour the sabayon over the fruit, then place under a hot grill for 1½-2 minutes, to lightly brown and glaze the surface. Serve at once.

GRATIN DES FRUITS D'HIVER

GRATIN OF WINTER FRUITS

Make a purée of blackcurrants with 250 g/8 oz black-currants and the juice of 1 lemon, sweetening to taste with caster sugar. Spoon the purée into individual gratin dishes.

Prepare a selection of winter fruits, such as apples, pears, clementines and blackberries, and arrange the fruits over the blackcurrant purée.

Prepare the champagne sabayon as for the Summer Gratin, then pour over the winter fruits. Glaze under a hot grill as before.

FRAGOLE AL BALSAMICO

STRAWBERRIES WITH BALSAMIC VINEGAR

The Italians have been using balsamic vinegar with straw-berries since the sixteenth century. Although it may seem an unlikely combination, the gentle acidity of balsamic vinegar does in fact bring out the flavour of even under-ripe and out-of-season strawberries that are sometimes lacking in taste. A delicious mascarpone and honey cream makes a delectable partner for these strawberries.

SERVES 4–6

1 kg/2 lb strawberries, halved
4 tablespoons caster sugar
4 tablespoons aged balsamic vinegar
sprigs of mint, to decorate

MASCARPONE CREAM
250 g/8 oz mascarpone cheese
50 ml/2 fl oz natural yogurt
2–3 tablespoons clear honey

Place the strawberries in a bowl and dredge with the caster sugar. Pour over the balsamic vinegar, toss well, then leave to macerate for about an hour, to allow the juices to run and the flavours to develop.

Beat the mascarpone cheese until smooth and creamy, then fold in the yogurt. Sweeten to taste with clear honey, blending well, so that the cream is smooth and light.

To serve, spoon the strawberries and their juices into tall wine glasses and spoon over the mascarpone cream. Decorate with sprigs of mint.

BRUSCHETTA DI FICHI AL MASCARPONE

TOASTED COUNTRY BREAD WITH FIGS, MASCARPONE AND HONEY

This is not really a dessert — more a wonderful sweet distraction!

SERVES 4

250 g/8 oz mascarpone cheese
1 tablespoon clear honey
2 tablespoons pine nuts, lightly toasted
4 figs, each cut into 8 sections
4 thick slices of Wholemeal Country Bread (see page 278)
sprigs of mint, to decorate

Beat the mascarpone cheese until smooth and creamy. Beat the honey into the cheese, so that it is just lightly sweetened. Fold in the toasted pine nuts and figs.

Lightly toast the bread on both sides. Spoon the mascarpone and fig mixture over the toast, then flash under a very hot grill for less than 60 seconds, so that the top of the cheese mixture is lightly glazed. Serve at once, decorated with sprigs of mint.

FRUTTI DI BOSCO GRATINATI AL MASCARPONE

GRATIN OF WOODLAND FRUITS WITH MASCARPONE

Smooth-as-velvet mascarpone cheese, served over a bed of fresh woodland fruits, then glazed under a hot grill, makes a heavenly dessert.
All red berry fruits contain high levels of vitamin C, while the mascarpone is a good source of both protein and calcium and has a lower saturated fat content than hard cheeses.

SERVES 4

125 g/4 oz raspberries
125 g/4 oz small strawberries
60 g/2 oz blackberries or blueberries
350 g/12 oz mascarpone
4 tablespoons granulated sugar
sprigs of mint, to decorate

Mix the prepared fruits together, then pile into individual shallow gratin dishes.

Beat the mascarpone until smooth, then spoon over the fruits. Sprinkle with granulated sugar, then place under a preheated, medium hot grill for 2-3 minutes, until golden brown and caramelized.

Serve at once, decorated with mint sprigs.

MELOCOTONES EN VINO SPUMANTE

PEACHES IN SPARKLING WINE

Simple yet elegant, this is one of my favourite summer desserts – ideal for a supper party with friends. Who could resist those juicy fresh peaches, served under a cascade of pink bubbles? My own preference is for sparkling rosé wine, but white is just as nice.

With their high vitamin C and beta-carotene content, fresh peaches are not only delicious, but nutritious too. With no added sugar, weight-watchers will be delighted to know that one peach contains only 30 calories, and let's not forget that a glass or two of wine a day is beneficial to good health.

SERVES 4

4 large juicy peaches
½ bottle sparkling rosé wine, well chilled

Blanch the peaches in boiling water for about 30 seconds, then carefully peel off the skins. Slice in half and remove the stones, then cut each peach into 8 segments. Arrange the peach slices in stemmed wine glasses, then pour over the sparkling rosé. Serve at once, while the wine is still bubbling.

ROTHAKINA KOMPOSTA

COMPOTE OF PEACHES WITH ORANGES
AND RASPBERRIES

The delectable juice-laden peach is here combined with oranges, raspberries and almonds, soaked in freshly squeezed orange and lemon juices with a hint of Cointreau. The fruits in this compote are served raw, so all the nutrients are wholly preserved, providing in particular excellent amounts of vitamin C.

SERVES 4

6 ripe peaches
freshly squeezed juice of 2 lemons
4 juicy oranges
45 g / 1¹/₂ oz cube sugar
3 tablespoons Cointreau
125 g / 4 oz raspberries
60 g / 2 oz split blanched almonds, lightly toasted
sprigs of mint, to decorate

Blanch the peaches in boiling water for about 30 seconds, then carefully peel off the skins. Cut the peaches in half, stone, then slice into segments. Brush the peaches all over with the juice of one of the lemons, then place in a serving bowl.

Rinse the oranges under cold water, then wipe dry. Rub the cube sugar all over the orange peel to extract all the zest. Squeeze the juice from 2 of the oranges and mix with the remaining lemon juice. Strain the juice over the cube sugar. Crush the sugar in the juices, then add the Cointreau and mix well until the sugar has fully dissolved.

Peel the remaining 2 oranges and cut into segments, discarding all the pith and segment membrane. Add the orange segments to the peach slices, then pour the Cointreau and juice marinade over the fruit. Place in the refrigerator to macerate for at least 1 hour, basting the fruit with the liqueur juices from time to time.

Just before serving, add the fresh raspberries and toasted almonds to the compote. Serve in pretty glass bowls, decorated with mint sprigs.

MACEDOINE DE FRUITS AU COINTREAU

SALAD OF FRESH FRUITS SOAKED IN COINTREAU

A fresh fruit cocktail makes a perfect conclusion to a meal – a selection of any of your favourite fruits will taste delicious soaked in this orange liqueur-scented syrup.

SERVES 6

4 juicy oranges, peeled, pith removed, then cut into segments, membrane removed
1 small pineapple, peeled, core removed and cut into chunks
250 g/8 oz strawberries, hulled and rinsed
2 large juicy peaches, skinned, stoned and cut into segments
1 small canteloup melon, peeled, seeded and shaped into balls using a Parisienne cutter (melon baller)
125 g/4 oz seedless black grapes
2 bananas, peeled and sliced

COINTREAU AND ORANGE SYRUP
2 oranges
60 g/2 oz cube sugar
150 ml/¼ pint water
5 tablespoons Cointreau

First prepare the Cointreau and orange syrup. Rinse the oranges under cold water, then wipe dry. Rub the cube sugar all over the orange peel to extract all the zest.

Place the cube sugar and the water in a small saucepan and bring slowly to the boil, stirring continuously until all the sugar has dissolved. Boil rapidly for several minutes until the liquid turns to a light syrup, then remove from the heat. Squeeze the 2 oranges and strain the juice into the sugar syrup, then stir in the Cointreau.

Prepare all the fruit except the bananas and place in a bowl. Pour the Cointreau and orange syrup over the fruit and place in the refrigerator to macerate for 1–2 hours, basting the fruit with the syrup from time to time. Shortly before serving, add the sliced bananas.

KHOSHAF

COMPOTE OF DRIED FRUITS WITH ALMONDS AND PISTACHIOS

Simple dried fruits can be transformed into a delicious, exotic-flavoured compote when marinated in freshly squeezed orange juice perfumed with rose-water and orange-flower water.
Dried fruits are highly concentrated sources of important nutrients, notably beta-carotene and the minerals potassium and zinc.

SERVES 4

125 g/4 oz dried apricots
125 g/4 oz dried peaches
175 g/6 oz dried figs
60 g/2 oz seedless raisins
600 ml/1 pint freshly squeezed orange juice
freshly squeezed juice of 1 lemon
1 teaspoon rose-water
2 teaspoons orange-flower water
175 g/6 oz mixed blanched almonds and pistachios

Place all the dried fruit in a large bowl and pour over the orange juice, lemon juice and scented waters. Leave to macerate overnight.

Add the mixed nuts to the compote and chill well before serving.

9
Bread

PAIN AUX NOIX

WALNUT BREAD

MAKES 3 × 500G/1LB LOAVES

30 g/1 oz fresh yeast or 1 tablespoon quick-acting dried yeast
125 ml/4 fl oz warm water
400 ml/14 fl oz milk
3 tablespoons clear honey
2 tablespoons extra virgin olive oil
375 g/12 oz stoneground wholemeal flour
375 g/12 oz strong plain flour
2 teaspoons sea salt
350 g/12 oz walnuts, finely chopped

Dissolve the yeast in the warm water and leave for about 10 minutes, until foaming.

Warm the milk gently over a moderate heat, then stir in the honey and olive oil. Leave to cool to room temperature.

Place the wholemeal flour, plain flour, salt and walnuts in a large mixing bowl and make a well in the centre. Pour in the yeast mixture and the sweetened milk, then gradually draw the flour into the liquid with your hands and knead to a sticky dough.

Turn out on to a lightly floured surface and knead well for about 10 minutes, until the dough is smooth and elastic. Return the dough to the bowl, cover with clingfilm and leave to rise in a warm place for about 1¹/₂ hours, until the dough has doubled in size.

Knock back the risen dough, then turn out on to a floured working surface and knead again for about 2 minutes. Divide into 2 portions, then place the dough in 2 lightly oiled 500g/1lb loaf tins. Cover loosely with cling-film, then leave to rise in a warm place for about 45 minutes, until again doubled in size.

Preheat the oven to 200°C/400°F/Gas Mark 6.

Bake the loaves in the preheated oven for 35–40 minutes, or until the loaves sound hollow when tapped on the bottom with the knuckles. Remove the loaves from the tins and leave to cool on a wire rack before slicing.

CIABATTA

OLIVE OIL BREAD

MAKES 2 LOAVES

20 g/³/₄ oz fresh yeast or 2 teaspoons quick-acting dried yeast
550 ml/18 fl oz warm water
1 kg/2 lb strong white flour
2 teaspoons sea salt
125 ml/4 fl oz extra virgin olive oil, plus extra for glazing

Dissolve the yeast in 150 ml/¼ pint of the warm water and leave for about 10 minutes, until foaming.

Place the flour and salt in a large mixing bowl, then make a well in the centre. Pour in the olive oil, yeast mixture and remaining water, then gradually draw the flour into the liquid with your hands, mixing to a soft, sticky dough.

Turn out on to a lightly floured board and knead well for about 10 minutes, until the dough is smooth and elastic. Glaze the inside of the mixing bowl with olive oil, then return the dough to the bowl, cover with clingfilm and leave to rise in a warm place for about 1½ hours, until doubled in size.

Knock back the risen dough, then turn out on to a lightly floured surface and knead again. Divide the dough into 2 portions, forming each into a round, flat ball shape. Place on a lightly oiled baking tray, spacing well apart, then cover loosely with clingfilm and leave to rise for a further 45 minutes.

Preheat the oven to 200°C/400°F/Gas Mark 6.

Brush the risen loaves with water, then using a very sharp knife, make 3 deep slashes across the top of each loaf. Bake the loaves in the preheated oven for 35–40 minutes, or until the loaves sound hollow when tapped on the bottom with the knuckles. Leave to cool on a wire rack before slicing.

PAN DE CAMPANA

WHOLEMEAL COUNTRY BREAD

MAKES 3 LOAVES

30 g/1 oz fresh yeast or 1 tablespoon quick-acting dried yeast
900 ml/1½ pints warm water
1½ kg/3 lb stoneground wholemeal flour
1 tablespoon sea salt
3 tablespoons extra virgin olive oil

Dissolve the yeast in 200 ml/7 fl oz of the warm water and leave for about 10 minutes, until foaming.

Place the wholemeal flour and salt in a large mixing bowl and make a well in the centre. Pour the yeast mixture, olive oil and remaining water into the well, then gradually draw the flour into the liquid with your hands and knead to a sticky dough.

Turn on to a lightly floured surface and knead well for about 10 minutes, until the dough is smooth and elastic. Return the dough to the bowl, cover with clingfilm and leave to rise in a warm place for about 1½ hours, until doubled in size.

Turn out the risen dough on to a lightly floured surface and divide into 3 portions. Form each piece of dough into a cylindrical shape, then place on lightly oiled baking sheets, spaced well apart. Cover loosely with clingfilm, then leave to rise in a warm place for about 45 minutes, until again doubled in size.

Preheat the oven to 200°C/400°F/Gas Mark 6.

Using a very sharp knife, make 4 deep slashes across the top of each loaf. Bake in the preheated oven for 35–40 minutes. The bread is ready if it sounds hollow when tapped on the bottom with the knuckles. Leave to cool on a wire rack before slicing.

PANE AL ROSMARINO E OLIVE

BLACK OLIVE AND ROSEMARY BREAD

MAKES 2 LOAVES

20 g/³⁄₄ oz fresh yeast or 2 teaspoons quick-acting dried yeast
550 ml/18 fl oz warm water
350 g/12 oz stoneground wholemeal flour
350 g/12 oz strong plain flour
2 teaspoons sea salt
4 tablespoons extra virgin olive oil
175 g/6 oz black olives
2 tablespoons finely chopped rosemary

Dissolve the yeast in 150 ml/¼ pint of the warm water and leave for about 10 minutes, until foaming.

Place the wholemeal flour, plain flour and salt in a large mixing bowl and make a well in the centre. Pour in the yeast mixture, remaining water and the olive oil. Gradually draw the flour into the liquid with your hands and mix to a sticky dough. Turn out the dough on to a lightly floured surface and knead well for about 10 minutes, until the dough is smooth and elastic. Return the dough to the bowl, cover with clingfilm, then leave to rise in a warm place for about 1½ hours, until doubled in size.

Blanch the black olives in boiling water for 10 seconds, then pat dry, remove the stones and chop finely.

Knock back the risen dough, then place on a floured working surface and knead in the black olives and rosemary. Divide into 2 pieces. Form each piece of dough into a slightly flattened round shape, then place on a lightly oiled baking sheet, spaced well apart. Cover loosely with clingfilm, then leave to rise in a warm place for about 45 minutes, until again doubled in size.

Preheat the oven to 200°C/400°F/Gas Mark 6.

Using a sharp knife, make 3 deep slashes across the top of each loaf. Bake the loaves in the preheated oven for about 30–35 minutes. The bread is ready if it sounds hollow when tapped on the bottom with the knuckles. Leave to cool on a wire rack before slicing.

Index

Greek egg and lemon soup, 17

scrambled eggs with sweet peppers, onions and tomatoes, 95

Spanish omelette, 86–7

ensalada de piperrada, 70

ensalada de sardinas de la Sierra, 42–3

ensalada Valenciana, 226

escalivada, 52–3

espinacas a la Catalana, 202

fennel: braised fennel, 204

grilled fennel, 206

roasted fennel, 205

salad of grilled fennel with tomatoes, 46–7

fettuccine alle erbe, 198

fettuccine nero alla Romana, 194–5

fichi al Barolo, 225

figs poached in red wine, 225

filets de maquereau au cerfeuil, 117

filets de saumon à l'aneth, 104

filets de saumon mistral, 122–3

finocchio al forno, 205

finocchio alla griglia, 206

finocchio brasato, 204

fish and shellfish, xv–xvi, 101–35

cleaning and boning, xx–xxi

deep-fried fish, 128

marinated fish kebabs, 118

Mediterranean fish soup, 28–9

see also individual types of fish

fragole al balsamico, 232

fraises au Champagne, 220

fraises au vin rouge, 220

fritto misto di mare, 128

fruit: compote of dried fruits, 240

gratin of winter fruits, 231

gratin of woodland fruits with mascarpone, 234

salad of fresh fruits soaked in Cointreau, 238–9

summer fruit gratin, 230–1

Valencian citrus fruit salad, 226

see also individual types of fruit

frutti di bosco gratinati al mascarpone, 234

funghi al forno alla Parmigiana, 208

gambas a la plancha, 116

gambas al ajillo, 81

game and poultry, 136–62

garlic, xiv

garlic croûtons, 35

garlic soup, 16

roast garlic purée, 209

gazpacho, 7

gratin des fruits d'été, 230–1

gratin des fruits d'hiver, 231

Greek country salad, 40

Greek egg and lemon soup, 17

Greek pilaf, 187

green beans tossed in olive oil and garlic, 207

ham: raw ham with black figs, 83

horiatiki salata, 40

huevos a la flamenca, 84–5